THE THIRD CENTURY

Twenty-Six Prominent Americans Speculate on the Educational Future

with an introductory essay by Nathan Glazer

Contents

IV — In Pursuit of the Millennium

V — The Third Century

VI — Epilog

About the Authors

STEPHEN K. BAILEY, a nationally known political scientist and analyst, is vice president of the American Council on Education. The author of numerous books on American politics and the Congress, Bailey headed the Maxwell Graduate School of Citizenship and Public Affairs at Syracuse University.

GEORGE W. BONHAM is editor-in-chief of *Change* Magazine, fund director of the Educational Change Foundation, and president of Science and University Affairs, a public policy organization.

HOWARD R. BOWEN is an authority on the economics of education, and the author, with John Minter, of widely publicized analyses of the financial status of private colleges and universities. Bowen served as president and chancellor of the Claremont University Center, where he is now professor of education and economics. He has held other leading positions in education, including the presidencies of the University of Iowa and Grinnell College.

ERNEST L. BOYER is chancellor of the State University of New York, the nation's largest system of higher education. He was also a member of former Vice President Nelson Rockefeller's Commission on Critical Choices and is a former president of the National Association of State Universities and Land-Grant Colleges.

ARTHUR M. COHEN is an associate professor of higher education at the School of Education of the University of California, Los Angeles. He also serves as director of the ERIC Clearinghouse for Junior Colleges and is a consultant to several community colleges.

2

K. PATRICIA CROSS is a research psychologist who holds a joint appointment with the Center for Research and Development in Higher Education at the University of California, Berkeley, and with the Educational Testing Service.

NATHAN GLAZER is professor of education and sociology at Harvard University and coeditor of *The Public Interest*. He is the author of *Affirmative Discrimination*, *The Lonely Crowd* (with David Riesman and Reuel Denney), *Faces in the Crowd* (with David Riesman), and (with Daniel P. Moynihan) *Beyond the Melting Pot*. He is also coeditor (with Daniel P. Moynihan) of *Ethnicity*.

EDMUND J. GLEAZER, JR., is president of the American Association of Community and Junior Colleges, a position he has held since 1958. He was previously president of Graceland College in Iowa.

SAMUEL B. GOULD is chancellor pro tem of the Connecticut Commission for Higher Education. He has been chancellor of the State University of New York and the University of California, Santa Barbara, and has served as president of Antioch College, the Institute for Educational Development, and the Educational Broadcasting Corporation.

THEODORE M. HESBURGH is president of Notre Dame University. He was chairman of the United States Commission on Civil Rights during the Nixon administration and has served on numerous major national bodies.

HAROLD HOWE II is vice president for education and research at the Ford Foundation. He was formerly United States Commissioner of Education, director of the Learning Institute of North Carolina, and superintendent of the Scarsdale, New York, school system.

RALPH K. HUITT has been executive director of the National Association of State Universities and Land-Grant Colleges since 1970, and was previously Assistant Secretary of Health, Education, and Welfare for Legislation.

MORRIS T. KEETON has been identified during much of his professional life with Antioch College. He joined Antioch in 1947, became its dean in 1963, and is currently vice president and provost.

CLARK KERR first came to national attention as the embattled head of the University of California. A distinguished labor negotiator, he was named chairman of the Carnegie Commission on Higher Education. He now heads the commission's successor, the Carnegie Council on Policy Studies in Higher Education.

LEWIS B. MAYHEW is on the faculty of Stanford University's School of Education and is the author of a summary volume on the reports of the Carnegie Commission on Higher Education.

JOHN D. MILLETT is an authority on the management of educational institutions. A political scientist and former professor at Columbia, Millett served as president of Ohio's Miami University before becoming chancellor of that state's board of regents. In 1972 he became head of the management division of the Academy for Educational Management.

FREDERIC W. NESS is president of the Association of American Colleges, and a former president of Fresno State College in California.

FRANK NEWMAN is president of the University of Rhode Island. He served as chairman of two federal task forces on the reform of higher education.

JAMES A. NORTON is chancellor of the Ohio Board of Regents. From 1965 to 1973 he served as head of the Greater Cleveland Association Foundation. He has also been a member of the faculty at Florida State University, Case Western Reserve University, and Oberlin College.

ALLAN W. OSTAR is executive director of the American Association of State Colleges and Universities.

CLAIBORNE PELL is a United States Senator from Rhode Island and the principal sponsor of the Education Amendments of 1972. He is the influential chairman of the Senate Subcommittee on Education, and was responsible for the legislation that created the national endowments for the arts and humanities.

CARL D. PERKINS is serving his thirteenth consecutive term in the Congress as the representative of Kentucky's seventh district. He has held the post of chairman of the House Education and Labor Committee since 1967 and has sponsored, among other bills, the Elementary and Secondary Education Act of 1965, the Vocational Education Act of 1963, and the Adult Basic Education Act of 1961.

ALAN PIFER has been president of the Carnegie Corporation since 1967. In his role as head of one of the most influential philanthropies in education, Pifer has supported the work of the Carnegie Commission, the

4

Carnegie Council, Christopher Jencks's work on inequality, and Charles Silberman's mammoth study of the American school.

ALBERT QUIE, ranking Republican member of the House Education and Labor Committee, was one of the principal authors of the Higher Education Amendments of 1972.

PAUL C. REINERT is chancellor of St. Louis University, a Catholic university with which he has been associated since 1944. Reinert has served on various Presidential commissions starting with the Eisenhower administration and is the author of the recent *To Turn The Tide*, a defense of private higher education.

DAVID RIESMAN is Henry Ford II Professor of Social Sciences at Harvard University. Among his many books are (with Nathan Glazer) *The Lonely Crowd* and *Faces in the Crowd*, and (with Christopher Jencks) *Academic Revolution*.

JOHN R. SILBER is the president of Boston University. He was formerly dean of the College of Arts and Sciences at the University of Texas.

Preface

In 1974, *Change* Magazine conducted a survey on leadership in American higher education. Some 4,000 college and university presidents, foundation executives, journalists, and government officials were asked to nominate those they considered the most important people in the academic enterprise. The results of the poll—a 44-person "Who's Who in Higher Education"—were published later that year. As might have been expected, the final list ranged from influential members of Congress to chancellors of the mammoth state university systems to distinguished scholars. (A few, such as Edward Levi, Elliott Richardson, and John Gardner, have since gone on to other endeavors.) The emphasis, however, was on the administrators—an indication, perhaps, that in the seventies, the academic manager has become the designated hitter of education.

The timing of the survey was not accidental. By the summer of 1974, the Watergate scandal had become a handy symbol of a pervasive loss of confidence in American leaders and institutions. For once, when people stopped to think of the "fabric of society," most of them realized it was not just an empty metaphor to be used loosely after dinner but something that actually exists, with a demonstrated capacity for unraveling. Higher education proved particularly vulnerable in this context, in large part because it may have been vested with too many hopes, saddled with too many responsibilities, and held accountable for too many solutions. Moreover, in the midseventies, most colleges and universities had only recently rediscovered their land legs after a decade of what is variously (and tediously) referred to as turmoil, turbulence, or tumult—terms that serve to mask the fact that much of academia still has only the vaguest notion of what the sixties may have been about.

With one decade safely in the charnel house, higher education turned to face the next, somewhat braced by what *Time, Newsweek*, and practically everyone else had discerned as a new quiescence on campus. Largely unanticipated, however, were the economic recession, the consequent specter of retrenchment not only on individual campuses but in whole cities, and the fact that vestiges of the sixties lived on in such things as attitudes toward education and work: Is college necessary? was the way Caroline Bird phrased it for mass-market consumption. To put it more precisely, many young people had begun to wonder whether they really wanted to become what Jacques Barzun called "that dreadful model of our age: the useful member of society who must be clothed in qualifications and armed with a license to practice."

With higher education facing one of its periodic watersheds, *Change* asked each of the 44 leaders to write an essay on his or her conception of the educational future, to ponder the dilemmas and directions for higher education in particular, and to carry the projections and prescriptions at least through the turn of the century. The result is the present volume. While we had originally intended to call it *Education in the Year 2000*, such a title now seems delimiting and artificial. As Alan Pifer has pointed out, there is nothing peculiarly special about that year except for a sort of magical, sentimental *fin-de-siècle* quality that has little to do with anything. *The Third Century* struck us as more appropriate, both because of the nation's bicentennial, and because the phenomena the contributors discuss have decidedly long-range implications. The essayists have their eyes on something more than "decisions and revisions which a minute will reverse." They are, after all, "decision makers," as the common phrase goes: people animated by responsibility for action and its consequences.

One cannot help but conclude that if tinkering with higher education is not a sufficient course of action for the next century, it is nevertheless the probable one. Whatever the conflicting utopias held up for espousal—however much one may be moved by visions of equality, lifelong learning, expanded access, a revitalized liberal arts, a compelling sense of purpose—what is likely is simply more of the same: the same slow progression through organizational plodding, the same fine-tuning of competing interests, the same (occasional) reinventing of the wheel. Not to mention the countless academic conferences as a shadowy surrogate for actual change. But as Nathan Glazer notes in his introduction—a point echoed by many of the contributors—there is always room for surprises. And the surprises may very well make room if there isn't.

—*Cullen Murphy*
Associate Editor
Change Magazine

Introduction:
The Business of the Future

Nathan Glazer

When 26 leaders of higher education—scholars, university presidents, foundation executives—have spoken of the future of American higher education, what, one may well ask, is there left to say by way of introduction? One thing that is left is to summarize the results: to take the variety of reflections and analyses, of viewings with alarm or with hope, and to consider what has been the result of this exercise, what is the current summary view, if one can be extracted? A second thing that is left is to take a larger view of the enterprise, a "sociology of projection," akin to the sociology of knowledge, and to consider who is worried about or optimistic about or even bothers to note what, and, as far as one can judge, why? A third thing that is possible is to consider the purpose of such exercises, the different ways in which they can be conducted—to engage in a kind of metafuturism, to analyze the problem of projecting the future as against engaging in the task directly. What does one learn from such exercises? Ideally, what can one learn? How does it, can it, relate to action? And a fourth thing that is possible is to join the fray oneself and to add yet a twenty-seventh comment on the future of higher education.

I

What then does an informed group of experts—the most informed, perhaps—see coming? The most prominent theme is the one we can sum up in the term "lifelong learning." Lifelong learning, of course, means many things: a higher proportion of adults attending colleges and universities; delay in the beginning of higher education and interruptions in it so that the individual, instead of running one main race, runs many smaller ones, responding to circumstance, need, interest; the use of institutions of higher education to provide new occupational training for those whose old occupations have become redundant, or for new tasks created by technology and society; and the use of such institutions to keep professionals up-to-date, and to teach leisure time pursuits and satisfy recreational interests (though only one or two of the group of experts foresee any great problem of a great deal of leisure time to be filled up—a common theme in projections of the social future in the 1950s and early 1960s). In addition to new functions for colleges and universities, "lifelong learning" also suggests a growth of higher education to off-campus locations, finding people where they are, relating education more intimately to their current occupations and locations. It also suggests a concurrent problem of standards and certification as higher education becomes many new things in many new places under differing kinds of arrangements.

It is this complex of elements that I mean to sum up with the term "lifelong learning," and this is the most commonly seen future for higher education. Lifelong learning is prominent because of a further perception, so common in these comments that even where it is not referred to directly or specifically it is in the background of the comments, taken for granted: Higher education is seen as having passed its peak in its ability to attract public funds, even if not as having passed its peak in its possible functions for society and individuals. This loss of higher education's ability to attract an increasing proportion of public funds or of the Gross National Product reflects the fact that higher education has passed its peak in other respects as well: in its ability to attract ever higher proportions of youth of traditional college age; in the advantages occupationally and in terms of income given by higher education; in public respect, owing perhaps to the student disorders of the late 1960s and early 1970s, or the failure of cadres drawn from higher education to deal effectively with foreign and domestic problems. (This last theme is so muted in these essays that it may be taken as mine rather than any of the participants'.)

Lifelong learning provides one alternative to the prospect of decline. There are a few who foresee, ingeniously, a complex interrelationship developing between higher education and those institutional sectors that are still expected to expand in the proportion of public funds they attract—health and environment being the two major possibilities. These relationships may mitigate the austerity foreseen as the proportion of budgets going to higher education remains stable or declines. Perhaps higher education can hitch on, through educational and research and retraining services, to the rising budgets that health and environment—and perhaps other areas—will attract. Another possible alternative to decline is suggested by the fact that the very slowing of economic growth as energy and raw materials become expensive and environmental pollution becomes a matter of increasing concern may itself require increasing investments in science and new technology from which higher education should benefit.

The prospect of extended lifelong learning is almost universally in these comments accepted as a good and worthy extension of the traditional functions of higher education, as well as a necessary and pragmatic one. Not that new difficulties are not foreseen: These are the problems of certification, standards, and credentials that Morris Keeton and James A. Norton in particular note, and there is John Silber's hilarious put-down, as we may call it, of the whole schmear. David Riesman cautions that the enterprise itself is a difficult and demanding one, as indeed are others which have perhaps been undertaken too blithely (e.g., higher education for ghetto youth with poor academic skills). As Riesman writes: "If one works with new constituencies, one must develop tests we do not yet possess for perseverance and willingness to endure failure—for both students and faculty; for to work with students who are not articulate, who come from homes and high schools with inadequate preparation, requires that faculty sustain themselves against the pedagogic despair likely to set in if one has started with the belief that everyone is capable of redemption through some form of higher education." (This comment should serve to remind us that up to now lifelong learning seems to attract in practice those who have already sampled and achieved in higher education, as against those who have not been reached by it, an early empirical finding from studies of efforts to extend higher education to new, adult constituencies in new settings that is not referred to in these comments.)

Alongside lifelong learning, and the coming period of austerity, a second major theme resonating through these comments is that of equality—the steady extension of higher education to those formerly limited in their ability to undertake it because of income, race, and sex (one can raise the question of what about those limited by taste or ability, but that scarcely comes up). Just about everyone who raises this theme foresees increasing egalitarianism in higher education; no one foresees a return to earlier limitations of income, race, and sex. But as against the simple celebration of the fact that the doors to higher education are now spread wider and will continue to widen (how can they not, when the campus of the future, as in the more spirited projections, will not have a specific location with doors or gates, but will be everywhere?), there are now to be heard many voices of caution, raising, most typically, the warning that it is necessary to balance the ideal of equality with a concern for quality. (Once again, the president of Boston University is scarcely cautious; equality endlessly extended, he tells us, simply becomes ridiculous.) There are suggestions—even from those most deeply involved in the push for equality, such as Father Theodore Hesburgh—that there has been some deficiency in the recent past in balancing equality and quality. Thus, Father Hesburgh: "Both as a member of the Commission on Civil Rights and the Carnegie Commission on the Future of Higher Education, I pressed long and fervently for better access to higher education on the part of those minorities so long denied equality of opportunity. While the task is still unfinished, we have succeeded beyond our initial hopes, and the machinery is in place for further success. As so often happens in human affairs, the good was in some ways the enemy of the better. Equality often came at the cost of quality...."

How quality is to be reconciled with equality is not very clear: None of the participants in this exercise who raise this question has any proposals. One approach might be the protection and strengthening of those institutions that maintain the best and highest standards: elite institutions of undergraduate education or of graduate education, those with the strongest and most highly respected programs, which select students with the greatest achievement and promise and provide the best facilities for study, teaching, and research—and which consequently spend more than other institutions.

The push for equality is not only one for equal access and equal achievement by individuals, it also gets transferred into a push for equal resources for all institutions, which inevitably means that it will be more difficult for concentrations of superior faculty, students, and research and teaching facilities to exist. Very few in the group are concerned for this aspect of equality, either to commend it or to consider the problems it raises for higher education. But David Riesman is concerned: "How can one justify maintaining the world resource of the library of the University of Illinois when Southern Illinois University is forced to let go tenured faculty?" And Harold Howe devotes a good part of his contribution to addressing the problem and making some practical proposals for dealing with it, proposals that seem to me to have merit and should be seriously considered (e.g., having the federal government undertake some part of the support of major university libraries, considered as national resources).

Another problem raised by the issue of "equality of institutions" is that of the survival, not necessarily of the most expensive ones, but of those that help create diversity, which are different from the norm in some respect. In particular, the problem is one for private institutions at a time when more and more of the funds for higher education, public or private, come from government, and at a time when government imposes for its mess of pottage more and more restrictions and requirements that limit diversity. Frederic W. Ness, president of the Association of American Colleges, is understandably concerned about this problem, as is Father Paul C. Reinert, chancellor of St. Louis University. Frank Newman, though president of a state university, is also deeply concerned. But it does not seem to trouble most of the participants.

This brings us to a third major theme: that of governmental intervention in college and university affairs, the danger of bureaucratic binding and limitation of educators. One should not exaggerate the prominence of this issue among the participants. While almost all of them see a future in which limited resources will be a problem, while more than half emphasize the importance of lifelong learning, and half place considerable emphasis on equality of access, I could count only a half dozen who raise this question. But those who bring up this issue raise it forcefully. If we had a measure of intensity (as one sometimes does in public opinion polling), I would say that while fewer raise the question of governmental intervention than speak of equality, the governmental issue is raised with much greater intensity. Undoubtedly, if we had a checklist for the participants rather than these free responses, more would agree this is a serious matter to take into account when considering the future of higher education. Frank Newman sees the possibility that higher education will be reduced by governmentally required bureaucratic limitations to the condition of timidity we associate (rightly, according to Harold Howe, who should know) with elementary and secondary education, which have for a long time suffered under many layers of governmentally imposed bureaucracy. No one who speaks of this problem sees any hope of mitigation of the trend of increasing governmental restrictions and requirements, though Frank Newman makes some useful proposals. (He suggests, for one, that government operate more through grants as incentives to induce change, less through requirements and regulations to impose it.) Alan Pifer does not see this as the same kind of problem. He points out that government grows because "there is an ever lengthening list of public needs which the American people consider government responsible for meeting." He dismisses a raft of promises by political candidates, asserting matter-of-factly: "There will, of course, be much rhetoric against big government, and perhaps some real attempts to reduce its responsibilities, but the general trend, whether we like it or not, will be in the other direction." It is hard to disagree: The only disagreement can be over whether we approve this development, and indeed it is possible that if enough people disapprove, the trend may be slowed, if not reversed.

A fourth theme is sounded by about half a dozen contributors, but mildly. This is that standby of the futurism of the past, new technology. What is surprising is the absence of Buck Rogers science fiction type of speculations and the modesty of the expectations or hopes (there are no fears) in respect to technology among those few who bother to refer to its possibilities. Indeed, technology generally comes in not as it has in most past utopias, to express an awestruck wondering as to what man can do, but pragmatically, to suggest how new technologies can help us cut costs by replacing that expensive form of higher education—putting a professor up before a handful of students—with more economical approaches.

Equally startling is the near disappearance of themes that one thinks would have played major roles in projections of the future of higher education 10 or 15 years ago. Thus, hardly anyone is concerned about providing an education for what was called, now more than 30 years ago, "one world." David Riesman notes sadly the "domestication" of higher education: Few students are concerned about learning about or doing something about the rest of the world. Allan Ostar and Father Hesburgh believe that education in foreign cultures should be (and therefore hope it will be) part of the higher education of the next century. Those are all the references I can find to the role of other cultures and countries in American higher education. The age of the Peace Corps, one is reminded, began 15 years ago, and it became a victim of Vietnam and the student radicalism of the late 1960s.

And hardly anyone comments on the student role in governance (an archaic term that seems to have come into common use to denote exclusively the governing of universities), and I count only three comments on governance in general, which deal with such issues as the greater demands on administration imposed by requirements for accountability (that *might* refer to a student role), the increasing role of federal and state government, and the new faculty roles coming in with unionization. An exception are George Bonham's interesting comments on the breakdown of the academic machinery. He seriously questions whether traditional academic governance schemes can survive into the third century of our national life. The role of the liberal arts in higher education gets even less attention: two comments, one of which is that it is not likely they can come back or maintain themselves in their old form, the other one of which says they should play a larger role—but it is Senator Pell who calls for that.

A scarcity of comments may indicate an issue that is no longer seen as important, or one that is not yet seen as important. I suspect education in foreign cultures, in leisure, the student role in governance fall into the first category. I would place in the latter category two further issues that receive little attention. Four contributors emphasize the importance of education in values. Whether that is a matter that will receive increasing attention, or whether the four comments are simply a reflection of American higher education's past, is a reasonable subject for argument. I think values will play an increasing role in discussions of higher education, but I may be wrong. There can hardly be any dispute that the fact that only three authors speak of collective bargaining and unionization reflects not the end of a storm but a coming one.

And finally, just about no one has any comment on student unrest or suggests that anything should be done to prevent it, or that the higher education of the future will in any way be shaped by it. So soon have the student disorders of the late 1960s and early 1970s been forgotten. One has to reach far to find any relevant comment. Lewis Mayhew does point out that it is clear higher education will not play the custodial role it has in the past. I agree. But I doubt from the past history of American higher education that student unrest will not return to become a major issue sometime before the turn of the century.

I have just given an example of what we might call "meteorological" prediction: Since it's happened before, it will happen again. I have no particular reason to suggest why it will happen again, except the one just given, that it has kept on happening.

And now to the "sociology of projection."

II

First, as is suitable for any sociology, a methodological note: Undoubtedly a different reader of this group of projections or predictions, or reflections for projection or prediction, or analyses that might serve projections or predictions (most of the contributions fall in the last two categories), would arrange the significant points differently, would find issues in them I have not noted, would not consider points I have mentioned (some with as few as two notices) worthy of mention. Undoubtedly, too, a different group of contributors would have been attuned to somewhat different issues.

With this caution, we can continue with a modest effort at the "sociology of prediction"—who says what, and why? There are not too many surprises. We do see specific interests reflected. The representatives of the community colleges are optimistic, of private colleges, gloomy. One contributor (Samuel Gould) at least quite directly takes the interest of all higher education and cautions the specific interests not to fight with each other and hamper the general interest in getting more for all higher education. It is not too surprising that of the three concerned for the future of diversity, one is the head of a Catholic college and another the head of the Association of American Colleges.

Nor is it too surprising, perhaps, that of the small group concerned about the problem of teaching values in higher education, two are the heads of Catholic institutions; a third is director of the American Association of State Colleges and Universities but has in mind fostering ideals of public and community service (he had just been to China); and the fourth is an elected official, Congressman Albert Quie, and his plea is the most forceful. He quotes and apparently has been influenced by Irving Kristol, who, had he been included, would, I imagine, have pronounced some kind of jeremiad on the present state and future direction of American higher education. (His role was taken by John Silber.) Albert Quie, an elected official, interestingly enough, is the only one in the entire group who mentions God, though one can assume the two Catholic leaders had the Deity in mind in making their pleas for transcendental values in higher education.

This brings us to the interesting issue of just who is making the predictions. The group was selected in a survey as leaders of higher education. The poll covered 4,000 university presidents, foundation executives, journalists, and governmental officials. Surveys inevitably introduce a certain bias in selection. One has to be known to be nominated, and thus it is understandable no student was included among the leaders. (One wonders if a student might have made it had this survey been conducted in 1969 or 1970.) People who respond to surveys, as against nominating committees, need have no concern for balance, racial or sexual. And so we have, as far as I can tell, no member of one of the minorities that are the particular concern of the Office of Civil Rights, and only one woman. Nor is there too impressive a representation—numerically speaking—from the most numerous group in higher education, the faculty. I count four contributors who are primarily faculty members, though of course others have been and may be again.

And taking into account the roles of those who are included, who are primarily administrators of individual institutions of higher education, of organizations of them, of foundations dealing with higher education, we can draw further conclusions: Clearly, for such leaders of higher education (I have already indicated there is considerable diversity among them, but now I speak in the large), the extension of higher education in some form to almost anyone capable of benefiting from it in any way is *the* major note for the future. (This is what "lifelong learning" and "equality of access" amount to.) There are only a few notes of caution sounded in this expectation or hope: that quality may be affected, that the task may be difficult (though that gets only one prominent mention). The major subordinate theme is the growing influence of government over higher education and its impact on creativity and diversity, but this is definitely a subordinate note.

It may be the business of the future to surprise us, as we are reminded by Alfred Whitehead, and it undoubtedly will. But the major themes that emerge from these 26 predictions march directly from the realities and concerns of the present. Will they disappear suddenly, as did the student unrest of a few years ago, in the next few years? It is hardly likely. Daniel P. Moynihan, summing up his insightful contribution on the American future for Nelson Rockefeller's Commission on Critical Choices, writes that Americans have two basic choices before them: how much government they want; and how much equality they want. The two of course go together. A choice for more equality means a choice for more government, and in the present state of American social and political forces, a choice for more government means a choice for more equality, too. I agree that these are the basic choices, and so it would appear do the contributors to this exercise in prediction. And they choose more of both, even if with some backward glances.

III

It is now time to consider what one wants from such exercises, what one gets out of them, how they should be viewed. To begin with, it is necessary to point out that hardly any of the contributors actually do *predict* a future for higher education. A bare prediction is in any case hardly meaningful. To predict, one must begin with a view of the present and add some basic assumptions. Having so begun, one may not get to any very specific prediction. But this is not basically what one wants from a group of highly informed individuals such as those who participated in this exercise. Using their assumptions, one could then call upon those skilled in the making of projections—which approaches more to science—to develop some specific and concrete pictures of what may be coming. This is what is done, for example, when one projects the future growth of a metropolitan area to assist planning or projects needs for a system of transportation, or what is done when, as has recently been attempted, but with a great deal of controversy, one projects key elements for the future of the entire world: population, income, use of energy, raw materials, and the like.

Something like this could be done for higher education, though it is understandable that it is in no way attempted in these brief contributions. What has been attempted is to provide the assumptions that would have to underlie any such broader effort. No futurist exercise is, or should be, a matter of straight-line projections. All straight-line projections eventually end up in absurdities. One is reminded of Derek Da Solla Price's projections of scientific growth, made in the 1960s, which demonstrated that it was impossible for the number of scientists, the quantity of research, the volume of scientific periodicals, and the amount of money necessary to support all of them to grow at the rates they had been growing for some decades. One could not imagine what, in those halcyon days, could happen to reduce this rate of growth. But something did happen to prevent those asymptotic curves reaching toward infinity from ever getting there.

Some of these assumptions needed for detailed projections must be assumptions as to what will change, as well as what will stay the same. This is the most difficult part of the art of futurism. It is easiest, and simplest, to simply project what is going on, even though we know it is the business of the future to surprise us. And indeed, it is helpful to have "surprise-free" projections, too—if nothing happens, this is how many students, teachers, buildings, we will need (or, currently, how many fewer).

But how does one work in these surprises? How does one discipline them so that, surprising as they are, they may well happen? For even if it is the business of the future to surprise us, we know we cannot stick in any surprise at all: The surprises in store for us should rest on things existent. Perhaps one can find the forthcoming surprises in strains in the system, elements of conflict in which the outcome is sufficiently doubtful that at least one outcome may properly be considered a surprise.

That seems like one reasonable approach to putting in surprises. As against science fiction, where just about anything can happen—say, finding samurai warriors on the moon—we would consider there are certain limits to surprises, established by the existent levels of population, science, technology, natural resources, and so on. Of course we would have to realize that no matter how carefully we placed our limits we might well be surprised by developments that transcended them. Could anyone in 1910, for example, have dreamed that a great percentage of the young men of England, France, and Germany would be dead by 1920, or in 1930 have dreamed that death camps would be established on a monumental scale in the 1940s? In other words, we need a dose of radical skepticism—as in Clark Kerr's fascinating account of how some very recent and apparently well-based expectations have been contradicted within just a very few years by actual developments in higher education.

There is a second point to be made about surprises in futurist scenarios: There is no way—and there should be no way—of removing our values from them. First of all, values will play a role in what happens, in what surprises come about; and those of us conducting such exercises might as well work out what happens if our values play a role in human choices, as long as these values are not so idiosyncratic that there is no chance of their being widely accepted. Secondly, the values we hold may suggest to us just what these less expected future developments might be. For example, it is those discontented with the radical secularism and scientism of the modern world who suggest, now and then, that substantial and new religious developments are possible. It is undoubtedly Daniel Bell's values that lead him to contemplate such possibilities in *The Cultural Contradictions of Capitalism*. And, surprisingly enough, in 1976 we elected a President who speaks about faith in God in a deeply personal way. Surprising developments are possible.

IV

And so, to possible surprises. We begin by noting a conflict—one of the few in these papers—between Howard Bowen's expectations as to the future relations between broadening access to higher education and equality of income and occupation, and Patricia Cross's. Patricia Cross believes—following the influential analysis of Christopher Jencks in *Inequality*, and one might add, along the same lines, the perceptive analysis of Raymond Boudon in *Education, Opportunity, and Social Inequality*—that we cannot expect broader access to higher education to reduce economic and occupational inequalities, or to affect the strong relationship between parental income and occupation and offspring's income and occupation. Howard Bowen, however, expects that with the increasing number of the college-educated, college will give decreasing advantages in jobs and incomes, and that this will lead to greater equality. We have two rather different perceptions, leading to different views as to what should be done, different expectations as to what will happen. Patricia Cross calls for higher education to make a greater effort to reduce inequality through education by means of a more individualized higher education, "education for each." Howard Bowen sees the simple broadening of access doing the job. But both either expect or hope the occupational and income advantage of higher education will be reduced. In any case, current trends indicate this advantage has already been reduced greatly (see Richard Freeman, *The Overeducated American*).

But now what happens to higher education when it no longer gives a specific and marked advantage to individuals? One would expect it to decline. Other institutions might move into a stronger position to undertake some of its present functions. State agencies and professional associations might move more strongly into the general area of credentialing. With the general depreciation of classroom education and with rehabilitation of apprenticeship and other forms of experience (a trend noted in these comments), more and more preparation for occupation might take place outside college classrooms: competency-based education. Higher education institutions hope still to have the job of evaluating this experience, but in view of their tendency to shy away from managing experience and to emphasize research and didactic teaching, why should they, rather than government civil service departments, or school departments, or bar associations and the like, manage to hold on to this task? One can, in other words, conceive of a more radical reduction of the scale and scope of higher education than any envisaged in these comments, one in which it is thrown back on its more specifically intellectual activities—which are, by the way, not prominently noted in these papers.

And other consequences would follow. Certain divisions within higher education would grow. One division would be based on the fact that there would undoubtedly exist institutions to which access was difficult and whose credentials did continue to give occupational and income advantages. We have had very little analysis yet of the specific income and occupational effects of types of institutions, levels of institutions. Our studies up to now are of higher education's effect in the aggregate. More detailed analysis might shake the current tentative conclusions that higher education has modest effects, at least for some institutions. The way people behave suggests they have passionate convictions in this regard, and they are not shaken by the current research—and future research might show they are right. Another division would be based on the degree to which institutions have involved themselves in the broadening of higher education into postsecondary education, the degree to which they have given up claims to distinction on the basis of intellectual authority and staked it on the broadness of their service.

The two splits might differentiate the same institutions, or different ones. But how would the general decline we project affect institutions of each type? Would decline affect more the service-oriented institutions and those that provided few economic advantages to their students, or the more traditional ones and those that provided substantial advantages? (The latter two would not necessarily be the same, but one could think of reasons why they might be.) When one considers that the former are more heavily public than the latter (once again, the relationship is not a close one), and that it is harder to foresee catastrophic declines in levels of support for public higher education than private (simply on the basis of the principle that established institutions with a claim to a budget are not easily disposed of in the public realm), then it may well be the more service-oriented and mass institutions that more effectively survive, while the traditional and the selective decline. Of course, it is possible the latter will be able to stake an effective claim to support on the basis of the differential advantages they offer, but I think the long-range chances are against the private and selective, except for a few strong institutions. In any case, the more rapid decline of the traditional and selective would be in harmony with the overall commitment to equality.

The institutions of higher education expect that they will be able to change enough to control the new approaches to occupational training, credentialing, and the like. The best guess is that they will—that is the surprise-free projection. A strong institution remains strong. And yet there are good reasons to think they may not. I believe the image of higher education in the eyes of the public is steadily weakening. One can see some direct signs of this weakening. The role of science and technology does not receive as unambiguous approval as it once did, from people in general, from educated youth. It is more essential than ever, but less liked, less admired. Is it a straw in the wind that one does not see evocations of college and university life in the mass media anymore— even though more people than ever are involved in it? Is it possible that college life is no longer glamorous, neither its football nor its various styles? Is it significant that the movies no longer even bother to engage in their wild caricatures of higher education and make fun of it? Is this a temporary ebb in the wake of the student rebellion? It is also true—one feels—that what is most central to higher education is not attractive to many youth. The best sellers on campus are Carlos Castaneda, astrology books, science fiction, *The Joy of Sex*, and their successors, and try as it may, higher education cannot really accommodate such interests.

Let us add to this admitted potpourri of signs of weakening the effects of a college teaching force shaped by the political ideas of the late 1960s and early 1970s. One reason that the American public supports higher education is that it expects it to teach patriotism and higher values, perhaps even religious values, to young people. That is one reason why all young people, the public believes, should continue their education. My guess is American higher education is less capable of performing this role than when William Buckley, in 1951, attacked the teaching on God and man at Yale. There is much talk now of retraining teachers to new subjects and new roles, so that philosophers and Romance language teachers, for example, might be competent in accountancy and marketing. One wonders whether this is possible, and I am rather skeptical when I consider how hard it is for most college teachers to get their PhDs in the first place, but hard as it is, it is easier than reshaping the present teaching force into one capable of teaching the values that the American public may demand as one outcome of higher education.

I have said that one's values inevitably enter into the surprises one may see coming. They can enter in two ways: One can use them to describe a future that rejects them, so as to warn people of the consequences (the bad future, as in Stephen Bailey's first set of projections, or in John Silber), or one can use them to shape a desirable future, to encourage people to cleave to it. The future I have described uses my values in the first way, but strangely enough even such a development might lead to the strengthening of the values I am committed to in higher education in some part of the enterprise. For if higher education is reduced in its general size and scope, it might simultaneously be restored to functions which cannot be taken away by state agencies, narrowly focused training institutions, professional organizations, and the like, which are candidates as sound as higher education for the expanded functions which postsecondary education hopes to perform.

There are, after all, old and permanent functions of higher education that it has in some sense retained now for centuries and which it is hard to see other institutions taking over. Clark Kerr, after his dose of radical skepticism as to the possibilities of projecting the future, reminds us of some of them (I am being selective, taking those most distinctive of higher education from his list): He speaks of higher education "as a source of ever more complex ideas,...a supplier of ever more needed social commentary as a basis for social reform,...as a preserver and enhancer of the ever expanding cultural heritage." We should never have thought it reasonable that higher education, pursuing these functions, would also have to become the marshaler, trainer, and sorter of all youth, something like the army in a system of universal service. We should never have expected that higher education could do more than provide opportunity in accordance with gifts—it was illusory to think it could ensure equality of income and opportunity and respect regardless of gifts or could eliminate the effects of heritage, or that it should. It may still be desirable on social grounds that there should be equality of income, occupation, and respect, but it is not higher education that can do it, and if it tries, it will become something quite different from higher education.

Thus it would seem two futures for higher education are possible. It can become the great sorter and trainer of all youth, with a mandate to ensure the greatest possible degree of equality, in which case "postsecondary education," the name now used in federal legislation, would be a better name for it, and the more traditional functions of higher education would be conducted in restricted parts of the institutional complex, perhaps furtively, perhaps with honor. But it is possible, and I think not unlikely, whether out of its own choice, or out of institutional incapacity to change, or out of governmental distrust, that higher education would continue doing what it has always tried to do in the past— preserve and pass on as best it can the cultural heritage (in which I include science), providing a base for some new thinking and research, laying claim to providing the specialized training for certain learned occupations, though always in conflict with other candidates for this task.

If higher education chooses or is forced into the latter course, we should realize, a good part of youth and the world will tell us they are not interested. And that is as it should be. They have other fish to fry, other functions to perform, and the university is not, and should not be, the world.

I
The Legacy of the Present

Small Steps
to a Larger Vision

David Riesman

Over the last decade or so, I have been involved in a number of efforts to think about the future, including the American Academy of Arts and Sciences' Commission on the Year 2000, and, more recently, the Carnegie Commission attempt to look into the future of higher education. But I have always done so with the uncomfortable feeling that even the most imaginative among us can do little more than extrapolate the past into the future, commonly our own more recent past. Whatever the future might be, my sense of the possibilities of historical discontinuity has been so strong that I have believed that most of us, myself included, are likely to prove very poor prophets indeed.

When I ponder historical discontinuity, two images—both of them connected with Japan—come to my mind: Since Hiroshima, the fear has never left me of the mushroom cloud and the destruction of the planet by nuclear weapons. In the 1950s and 1960s I made it a practice to ask students whether they had fantasies or nightmares of such destruction. During the Vietnam War agitation of the late 1960s, such concerns were rare to the point of nonexistence: Antiwar Americans could apparently think of only one issue at a time, just as more recently many could think only of Watergate or of Israel or of what in comparison with nuclear weapons seem relatively manageable ecological considerations of pollution and population. Because of the looming dangers in the Middle East, there is now some renewed concern over nuclear weapons, but it is insufficient to restrain the many enemies of détente with the other major nuclear power, let alone to organize efforts to limit nuclear proliferation and support further measures of arms control that look toward eventual elimination of planet-destroying armaments.

The other episode connected with Japan is not a futuristic fantasy but an historical episode, namely the extraordinary story of the Meiji Restoration. A group of mostly ascetic and communally minded samurai leaders came to the fore. They drew from various strands of Japanese traditions (including the small Dutch enclave at Nagasaki) the strength and the capacities in a previously insulated country to avoid Western domination by syncretistic adaptation of Western learning. A number of these leaders had not been previously mobilized: Unafraid of exercising authority, uninhibited by egalitarian sentiment, they dared to appear as traitors to some of their own countrymen and fellow samurai by immersing themselves in Western science and learning. They faced a relatively homogeneous population, still influenced by a Confucian ethic of loyalty to the extended family, which could be mobilized on behalf of larger corporate groups and the nation-state itself. Literate, hard working, immensely skillful, the participants in this revolution from the top allowed the Japanese to "overtake and surpass" their Western models in diverting income to reinvestment and in maintaining a degree of restraint in the general population which the Soviet Union, a more insecure society, has scarcely been able to achieve either through terror or its periodic mitigation. (Indeed, the nonviability of the Soviet Union, with its multi-ethnic fragments and "People's Democracies" always ready to tear loose, beneath the seeming strength of nuclear and other armaments and modern industrial development, is one of the reasons I fear for the world future, and put détente above all other strategic and compelling moral considerations.)

The United States was never so insulated as Tokugawa, Japan, although its nineteenth-century deference to European models of high culture, lasting well into our current era, was one lever for developing a small group of research-oriented universities built on what was believed to be the German model. When successful, it managed to combine the philanthropic support of loyal undergraduate alumni with growing support from state and federal governments for the more esoteric branches of scholarship. Yet in comparison with Japan, America has remained, despite this traditional window vis-à-vis Europe, more provincial and self-preoccupied: more cosmopolitan in one sense, but monolithic nonetheless. Our educated elites, now deprecating such former indices of unrelenting growth as GNP and population, have not yet found immersion in a world economy and world culture a way to replace the former self-confidence. These elites have become less ethno-centric, less complacent and self-confident, in many cases as a result of the trauma of the Southeast Asian wars. Justified pride in our educational and cultural achievements has not substituted for the loss of the older sources of American self-assurance.

After my apocalyptic fashion, I began saying to complacent liberals and euphoric radicals in the late 1960s that the time was soon coming when the United States would receive not its annual increment of oil but the same amount as the previous year; and then we would elect George Wallace President. We would not be able to endure austerity and restraint imposed upon us by our sinking position in a world economy in which we were competing with peoples whose expectations of "meaningful work," endless abundance, and ever-increasing social services were more modest than ours. When the oil embargo came—sooner than I had anticipated—the result was not samurai-like restraint but increasing feelings of grievance and envy endemic to Americans—for feeling aggrieved is a way to justify one's own claims—and a search for villains, whether among the oil companies, the Arabs, the Jews, the ever-maligned politicians, or bureaucrats. (In looking for national leaders, we seem preoccupied with senators who have run a staff of a dozen, when we should be looking to governors or mayors or executives who have run large organizations—men and women whose narcissism has not led them away from the harness either of a political party or a collegial organization.)

To turn from ground to the educational figure, the major American colleges and universities suffer from a climate of depression at once psychological and budgetary. Yet there remains in our educational efforts an old American legacy reflecting previous relative success and affluence: It is the belief that good things are compatible with each other, and that one does not need to make difficult choices as to which good things any particular institution or group of institutions will take as its own mission. As I have studied experiments in higher education that have been undertaken from the late 1950s to the early 1970s, I am reminded again and again of the unwillingness to sacrifice one value for the sake of pursuing others. To illustrate: I believe that to develop methods of preparing graduate students for careers as college teachers requires an extraordinary inventiveness, department by department, an inventiveness that would take into account the whole of the life cycle as this differs between such "beauty queen" fields as mathematics and such "wisdom" fields as history or political science.

Change Magazine itself has contributed to the climate in which it is widely believed among dissenting academics (who in many experimenting institutions make up the vocal majority) that so-called interdisciplinary programs require principally goodwill and rejection of stuffy departmentalism. Yet to create a single good interdisciplinary program, whether in teaching or in research, is the most arduous and never-ending kind of intellectual work; subspecialties develop and become new disciplines, new boundaries are formed—indeed, often required as protective tariffs for infant educational enterprises. However, the same institutions that have given themselves the mandate of becoming interdisciplinary or nondepartmental tend also to be those that have taken seriously their responsibility to racial and class injustice, and as if that were not enough, to reducing hierarchy within the institution and tinkering endlessly with more or less participatory governance.

This belief in the compatibility of our ideals rather than the necessity for individuals and institutions to choose and concentrate their efforts is already leading, well before the year 2000, to a paradoxical alliance between educational innovators from the pedagogic left and tax-conscious officials and publics from the political right. (This alliance was already adumbrated in the late 1960s when, for example, Governor Ronald Reagan could agree with spokesmen of the Free Speech Movement that Berkeley had a faculty who did not do enough teaching and were too much involved in research and consulting, a destructively philistine reaction to the undoubted problems of undergraduate, especially lower-division, education in great universities, though Berkeley nevertheless had attracted these same students and, as many studies showed, satisfied them in academic if not cultural terms.)

The combination of material success and a surviving secularized puritan tradition has made Americans in the past extraordinarily sanguine and evangelistic, as much about the limits to change as about the limits to growth. Nowhere has this been more evident than in the so-called nonprofit sector, where euphoric enthusiasts have made extravagant claims as to who could be taught what at whose expense. In earlier epochs we could afford as a nation, if not as individuals, the defeat of excessive hopes and the bankruptcy of institutions because we were living on an ever-rising plateau and could start all over again on a new wave of reform. Currently, the situation is far more grave. I believe that in education we are faced with the same cycle that the poverty programs of the Lyndon Johnson era experienced: To gear up Americans to volunteer their money and labor requires making excessive claims, minimizing long-run costs, and then often blaming social science skeptics for being the messengers who point out the failures of which many have long since become aware.

What seems to me required if educational institutions are to meet the dilemmas already upon us are "un-American" combinations of skepticism with faith, fatalism with pragmatic activism. What we see instead is a diminishing but still influential number of euphoric reformers who are so convinced of the failure of traditional higher education that they are sure that doing away with elements of its structure, such as course credits, grades, and departments, will automatically produce the benefits now claimed for nontraditional study precisely for the more deprived part of the population, whether teen-agers turned off from books or older people who missed their chance the first time around. And these are the individuals who most need structure and support, preferably, I would think, in residential settings. Many institutions I have examined that embark on experiments with a staff sharing the "negative identity" of being against prevailing norms have discovered that to do more serious education for less money is an unlikely outcome of their frequently heroic overwork. Affluence can no longer be counted on to bail us out of past experimental disasters and allow us to start others blithely. I have feared for years an educational backlash, comparable as just suggested to the boom-and-bust cycle of the poverty programs of the last decade.

I believe that carefully supervised off-campus work can greatly enlarge educational possibilities for undergraduates and graduate students alike. Nongraded courses can encourage students to experiment with areas in which they feel weak or inadequate. Mature adults can bring to the campus a diversity far greater than the heterogeneity of any group of adolescents—who so often in the elite colleges complain about their supposed homogeneity and seek to recruit the deprived in part out of guilt and in part out of exoticism. But if one works with new constituencies, one must develop tests we do not yet possess for perseverance and willingness to endure failure—for both students and faculty; for to work with students who are not articulate, who come from homes and high schools with inadequate preparation, requires that faculty sustain themselves against the pedagogic despair likely to set in if one has started with the belief that everyone is capable of redemption through some form of higher education. Furthermore, all these experiments involve long-run costs that the initiators are unlikely to appreciate: cumulative costs for individual careers, and the danger of exhaustion of hope and energy for the institutions themselves.

As I have said, it is an all too American belief that all reforms are compatible and that all students (or indeed faculty) can be redeemed if one only tries hard enough. (It is ironical that these same attitudes are often shared by reformers who in their politics are vociferously anti-American—which, as I have indicated, does not mean that they are truly world-minded—believing that if the United States is no longer the City on a Hill for the world, it must therefore be the imperialist contamination of the world—vanity in reverse.)

I have observed that a good many educational reformers are or once were members of religious orders or Protestant seminarians. Some have found a new vocation, for example, substituting the encounter group for the monastery. Disparaging the "merely" academic, they seek to be pastoral vis-à-vis students, while at the same time egalitarian: a dilemma of authority that is seldom resolved and sometimes leads to a conflict with family life for the no-longer celibate who move in on students or vice versa without the capacity to stay young forever.

I have made clear my fear that some extraordinarily useful innovations will be discredited, as the change-minded going in one direction combine in an often unconscious coalition with the budget-minded going in the other. Each is at odds with the still-entrenched departments in the major training centers for faculty.

Both the change- and the budget-minded share another American complacency: They believe that if only the proper legislation can be passed or the proper mandates issued, people will be found to develop the new programs that are required. On the part of the budget-minded, this means that every state must possess career officials in higher education who are capable of, in Martin Trow's terms, distinguishing the public and the private life of complex institutions without destroying the latter because of funding formulas created for the former. In the case of the change-prone, they generally underestimate the human finesse, technical skill, and dedication required to create something new and to make an assessment of it; this would be so even if there were many more summer workshops and Danforth-type resources for faculty development. Something on the order of 600,000 faculty members in American colleges and universities have to be thought about when one considers the impact of changes. As with Medicare, which created a demand for health services before there were adequate supplies and thus created inflation where it did not create fraud, educational programs are instituted that require scarce and expensive talents to develop and to judge—on the egalitarian and happy assumption that everybody really possesses the necessary talent, only waiting to be released from the tyranny of Carnegie units and credit hours. Furthermore, many of these developments ignore the anxieties students naturally feel at this time vis-à-vis their occupa-

tional futures, which lead them to hesitate to embark on programs
that postbaccalaureate schools or employers may regard as preten-
tious ways of goofing off.

The United States now competes in a world economy for which
it is unprepared; we have become postindustrial in spirit before
we can afford it, and many of our finest intelligences are turning
against technology, leading to an intranational class warfare between those who want jobs and those who want amenities. In our
more selective colleges, I witness a depressing brain drain into law
and to a lesser degree medicine, seen as individualistic callings
where "nobody will be the boss of me," a fallacious estimate,
while avoiding work in high-technology corporations or in the sciences and engineering, which tend to remain "first generation" callings that (as the military does also) draw from the periphery of
cosmopolitan America. The belief that we are becoming a service
society, which I myself once held, has been gravely overdone; accordingly, many of our ablest young people are being misled. I see
many people who want to enter the legal profession because of its
veto power over construction of highways, nuclear reactors, or
other environmentally questionable enterprises. But very few
wanting to enter those enterprises do so in the hope of incremental
change from within. Certainly very few people want to be "leaders," who are so often targets for ungenerosity, as the attitudes of
faculty toward academic administrators, or the population toward
the politicians we elect, demonstrate. (In our large managerial corporations, the office holders are not leaders, but on the whole
rather timid men, stewards for the enterprise, anything but founders of dynasties; and when we do have such dynasts, as in the
case of the Rockefellers, we seek to pull them down to common
size, a posture many of them assume *ab initio*.)

In the areas where we have remained world leaders, namely, in
science, scholarship, and the arts, I fear a similar leveling process
is already under way. The American middle class in the East has
now made the discovery pioneered in the South and the West that
it is possible to shift the burden of one's children's college education, by the regressive patterns of state taxation, to the poor and
sometimes the very rich, and private education becomes not only
expensive but increasingly as "unnatural" as single-sex education
has become. Thus, with a few fundamentalist exceptions, the major liberal arts colleges and private research universities are threatened as never before with financial extinction, caught between the
inflationary rise of costs and expectations and the inability in a
populist democracy to select and support a few "centers of excellence" as the seed corn of high culture. But the situation is no bet-

ter with the major research-oriented state universities. How can one justify maintaining the world resource of the library of the University of Illinois when Southern Illinois University is forced to let go tenured faculty? How can we retain the musical distinction of Indiana at Bloomington when Indiana at Terre Haute is suffering? And how can the federal government justify providing merit fellowships, research grants, and other efforts to sustain "centers of excellence" when this means curtailing some postbaccalaureate programs and maintaining the inevitably "unfair" status quo of academic distinction?

Above all, how can the federal and state governments prevent what I see as the "domestication" of the United States with the loss of the National Defense Education Act Fellowships at the same time that foreign language requirements are being abandoned almost everywhere, and domestic concerns loom preeminent among many of our most idealistic young people? As a reaction against the Cold War and other (in my judgment) dubious motives for supporting attention to countries outside our borders, when the Peace Corps is looked upon with suspicion at home as well as abroad, even the anti-imperialist young, the anti-American Americans who are apt to travel abroad a great deal, count on speaking English to individuals who, because of the distinction of our universities and the prevalence of our technology, are willing to learn our tongue. Foreign area studies are among the first cuts when broad budgetary austerities threaten, just as foreign aid to the starving in West Africa is no longer defended by Cold War rhetoric, and only barely sustained. How can we justify spending scholarship aid to bring foreign students here vis-à-vis the claims of the mobilized cadres of deprived, and their white patrician sponsors, within our own society? The Americans who do care about other lands tend to be those with ethnic ties, such as Zionist Jews or, more rarely, pro-IRA Irish-Americans—hardly an optimal situation for creating any kind of world order or maintaining any universal standards of world culture. (The interest of American blacks in Africa is as yet extremely limited even among the educated, as was evident to those of us trying to arouse interest in the Biafran secession movement in its initial stages, although this is rapidly changing.)

The Japanese had the enormous advantage in the Meiji Restoration that they could follow the lead of a shifting roster of Western countries (America for know-how, Germany for education, France for culture, England for polity) as they themselves moved into the forefront of modernity in technology and the arts. But the United States has been in the awkward position of having no models of its own except repeated revivalist movements of our own conflicting ideals of liberty and equality. We do not yet know whether it will be possible to live amicably in a postaffluent, highly individualistic society. We do not yet know what sort of education such a society would find socially useful and individually creative. My guess is that it would be a great variety of forms of education, in and out of formal institutions, with some educational tasks far better done by Xerox or Polaroid than by Harvard or Long Beach State University. Our ignorance is overwhelming, which makes our claim that we know what to do so preposterous and self-defeating. Thus, when over the years I have talked with educational reformers with messianic visions, I have had the temptation to beg them to "think small," to take some difficult incremental step along but a single dimension.

And yet it is not enough simply to "think small." One has to take small steps with an eye toward a larger vision of Spaceship Earth, aware not only of its finiteness but also of the fact that nationalism (and within America, its ethnic variants) remains among the strongest ideological powers in the world, capable, as I suggested at the outset, of destroying that world with nuclear weapons. At the same time, the history of the human race exhibits extraordinary resiliency and adaptability. The small steps we take must be guided by the larger vision, as the navigators of an earlier era guided themselves by the North Star while adapting their momentary seamanship to the winds and currents around them. My own vision of a future world is of individuals rooted in a culture, in a calling, even in some instances a tribe, who nevertheless are capable of rising to universalistic judgments of quality, whether embodied in great works of art, architecture, and science, or in great individuals whom we will encourage as our leaders (developing especially among Americans a needed talent for followership short of idolatry), a world in which leveling has not occurred, as premised on envy and *ressentiment*, but in which individuals are encouraged to stretch themselves to the limit of their abilities and are responded to in terms of their highly idiosyncratic and quite unequal needs.

Can we "think small" about the enormous variety of patterns of postsecondary education (including truly higher education) that will get us a little nearer to such a vision rather than enclosing us within the great American parish that is pulling down the secular cathedrals of its distinguished universities without filling up the miseries of its deprived, let alone the wretched of the earth?

A Disease With a Patient

Samuel B. Gould

It is fashionable these days to speak gloomily about everything, and education is bound to come in for its share of the general hand wringing. That education is changing (as it always is), that some of the changes are caused by external pressures (as always), and that some of the changes are upsetting to the general academic equilibrium (inevitable but not necessarily dire)—all of these are troubling because they add further insecurity to an already insecure establishment. Given such circumstances, the safest course to follow in the short run is to do nothing in the hope that "this, too, shall pass away."

My own feeling, however, continues to be one of strong optimism linked with determinism. I still believe we are entering a new and more fulfilling era for higher education, different in its characteristics and even eventually in its motivations, but rich in potential effectiveness. And I still believe that today's baffling problems and trials can, in the long run, lead to a stronger, more comprehensive, more interrelated set of educational systems than those with which we are currently familiar. The real and immediate questions concern not so much what the future will turn out to be as what we truly want it to be and how we propose and plan to get there.

I am increasingly aware that I am in a strange, even paradoxical, situation. One side of the paradox is that during the past five years I have functioned in the educational world without a college or university base. This has taken me off the battlefields of earlier years. It has made me wonder whether today's problems are actually so much more difficult than yesterday's or whether my dogged optimism is in fact a rather advanced form of senile folly. The other side of the paradox, however, is that during those same five years I have had the opportunity, at home and abroad, to examine the educational scene and to move about within it with a broader, more objective point of view. I have had no personal ax to grind other than that of wishing to see higher education thrive and fulfill its promise. Such opportunity has probably not made me wiser but it has sharpened my reactions. I find the picture much different under these new circumstances, different in perspective and clarity. I now suspect that far too many of our current difficulties we have forced upon ourselves. And as my suspicion grows, I recall the words of Sir William Osler, the eminent Canadian clinician: "It is much more important to know what sort of patient has a disease than what sort of disease a patient has."

It is a truism that the patient in this instance has a multiplicity of images. One can call out any of a number of names and be sure of a response: community or junior college; four-year liberal arts college, private or public; university, private or public; urban university; land-grant college; vocational training and education; career education; specialized undergraduate degrees; graduate education; professional education; continuing or adult or extended or recurrent education. Higher education represents different things to different people not only in what it is but in what they believe it should be. But, presumably, it is always "higher" and therefore worthwhile to whoever has a real desire to know more or to be able to do something better. We have always regarded this diversity as a great positive factor and we remind each other of it again and again.

With such multiplicity of images, however, a less fortunate or less attractive characteristic emerges as well, namely, an inability to interpret higher education to the American people in some sort of unified way. Diversity leads us to encourage and maintain several kinds of divisiveness among ourselves. We even appeal to the public to take sides. In so doing, we cause confusion and uneasiness among our various constituencies and weaken our potential for support. We speak endlessly about the virtues of diversity in education, but every aspect of that diversity seems to be in an adversary relationship to every other.

For example, although we have established rather well the conviction that different sorts of education are appropriate for learners with differences in abilities and objectives, at the same time we adopt an attitude of mere toleration for patterns of learning that do not reflect those at our own particular institution. Sometimes it is the private college against the public; sometimes the community college against the four-year institution; sometimes the liberal arts against career education or formal against nonformal learning. But whatever the issue, there has been far too much partisanship in higher education and far too much ill will in its expression. This has created the impression that higher education does not have its house in order as it turns for support to its citizenry, whether through public or private sources. Despite our pious declarations that we see benefits in every citizen's being better educated, we make arbitrary classifications of quality that reflect our prejudices against anything that strays from the formal, the familiar, the long-accepted. This is the message that reaches the public and it puzzles them.

The message that should be reaching them is altogether different. It is that the house of learning has many mansions; that the doors to all should be open to those qualified to inhabit them; and that the furnishings and styles are necessarily as different as the dwellers. There is nothing antithetical in the existence of these mansions side by side, or in the actual or potential neighborliness of those who teach and learn within them. They represent the many resources available to the learner, all of them important, all of them deserving of support when they are carefully and appropriately constructed.

There can be little doubt that this message will assume even greater importance during the next several decades as the consequences of today's changing patterns of learning become apparent. These have to do with more flexibility of access, more variety in teaching methods, different kinds of rewards, new philosophies relating to funding, more concern for individual need—a confederacy of alternatives, some proven, some not. These patterns will continue and so must be reckoned with. No self-respecting educator and, indeed, no lay person would countenance their encouragement if they are shown to be lacking in quality. They must thus be carefully monitored.

But the real questions about such patterns are related to where they belong and whether they will add still another element of divisiveness to the many others. They lead us to the even larger questions of what fits under the rubric of "higher education," and how there can be some sort of clear, unemotional, and unprejudiced interpretation of what all of education is designed to provide. The answers may lie in new alignments and new nomenclatures for a good deal of what we now casually call "higher." They certainly call for new understanding and mutual respect among the various segments of education. Otherwise, today's confusion and acrimony will merely be compounded.

To speak of new alignments and new nomenclatures raises a set of possibilities so far generally neglected and unexplored. It is easy enough to identify kindergarten and elementary education, and even secondary education poses no great problems. But a vast proliferation occurs immediately thereafter when we talk of postsecondary education, and it relates not only to levels of learning but to purposes and objectives as well.

The steady increase in the number of alternative programs as well as in the number and types of people availing themselves of them adds still another component. We are already at the point where of all those seeking to fulfill postsecondary learning needs, about half are turning to alternative means outside the formal educational system. Is this to be welcomed or deplored? Does it represent types of education our formal system prefers to ignore? Is it perhaps wiser for colleges and universities to stand aloof from these expressed needs and limit themselves to serving students of traditional college age? Will college-age students be tempted by alternative possibilities? If so, why? Do we face a telescoping of the formal educational system as a result of this competition, or of the lowering of the birthrate, or of new economic stresses? Do we need to create a new and separate sector of postsecondary education with a different set of rewards?

Questions such as these indicate that although one might at first dismiss as inconsequential how we classify types of learning and how they are or should be interrelated, considerable importance attaches to them. Take, for example, the concept of lifelong learning.

Lifelong learning, so vital a part of the American educational dream, is spoken of now as though it were something new. But, of course, it is not new at all; it merely keeps on being rediscovered—and reforgotten. The other day, for example, while using my old Webster's unabridged dictionary, I found myself for some reason reading its preface. William Allan Neilson wrote it 41 years ago, and this is part of what he says:

> Within recent years there has been a new emphasis on adult education. In spite of the multiplication of schools and the great increase in numbers of students in colleges and universities, it is more and more recognized that education does not and cannot end with attendance at institutions of learning. It is a lifelong process, in which the school or college is chiefly important in supplying tools and teaching how to use them. For the conception of the educated man as a finished product is being substituted that of the intellectually curious person, aware of the vast-

ness of human ignorance but challenged by the light that is continually being thrown, through scientific research and other activities of the human mind, upon all aspects of the universe.

If we chose, we could go much further back into the past and discover statements that antedate Neilson's by decades or centuries. We might even go back to some of the original concepts of how learning takes place, concepts espoused and practiced by people like Socrates or the Talmudic scholars. They all attest to the virtues of lifelong learning as an essential part of any person's growth.

This concept is one, therefore, that we are still eager to see accepted, strengthened, and widely adopted, and a good deal of our future effort should be concentrated on the ways and means of encouraging precisely that. But we have moved in this direction not only tentatively but unsteadily.

One first move academics could make is that of better knowing and understanding one another, and similarly, of better knowing and understanding those who are outside our world but nevertheless influence it. Familiarity does not always breed contempt. In new interrelationships we may find to our amazement a new respect for what others are accomplishing or trying to accomplish.

Lord Ritchie-Calder, writing in the *Center Magazine*, describes a group of young scientists at Oxford and Cambridge in 1926 who decided that "in their preoccupation with science, they were losing touch with the world outside," and formed a dining club, the "Tots and Quots" (*Quot Sententiae Tot Homines*—"As many opinions as there are men"). This was designed to show that even though they were scientists, "they were on speaking terms with the humanities." They met as a monthly dining club on neutral ground in London. They invited outsiders: politicians, diplomats, and divines. They were concerned even then with the social relations of science, with the use, abuse, and nonuse of science.

We do little of this sort of thing in America, and we rarely do it gracefully. Perhaps it is our sense of insecurity that is the reason, and perhaps it is that same sense of insecurity that keeps us from doing what we should about education generally: taking the initiative in assessing the effects upon education brought about by external changes in society, and taking similar initiatives in making education what we think it ought to be. We seem uneasy in the brittle and shifty public relations world that surrounds and includes us about being caught with a conviction from which we cannot hastily retreat, a point of view that has no convenient hedge, or a commitment that is anything but conditional. Categorical imperatives in education are not just rare; they are nonexistent.

Higher education in the next quarter century may develop like a child growing up over whom we, as parents, have had responsibility but no control. The result may be a monster or a passive nonentity or even a prodigy. The accidents attached to bringing up children are well known to us all. But the future of higher education also has the possibility of being based on firm convictions as to what it should be and how the achievement of clearly stated goals may be reached. And these should be goals and actions that originate in a unified sense of purpose within the academic world, stimulated by mutual respect, by a similar respect for external forces, and by mutual concern for the individual learner at any postsecondary level. Furthermore, they should be goals and actions that have their birth in internal initiatives, initiatives that represent more than reactions to temporal crises or pressures. What we need most, if we are to be strong in our educational position, is the courage to close ranks and take charge.

En Attendant 2000

Clark Kerr

The year 2000 will arrive at its own pace. The effort to look at it in advance involves, in part, curiosity and, in part, a hope to change its contours or at least to adapt in advance to its anticipated constraints. Realization of either part of that hope will deflect 2000, however slightly, from what it would otherwise be. In response to both the curiosity and the hope, some things can be said with a degree of assurance.

The persistence of heritage. Lord Eric Ashby once wrote that we cannot know "what the environment of tomorrow's world will be like" but "we already know what its heredity will be like." And heredity in higher education is a particularly strong force. The universities of today can draw a direct line back to Bologna and Paris and Oxford and Cambridge. Compared with universities, even religious institutions have changed more, and political and economic institutions incomparably more. So the first observation is that higher education in the next 25 years, in all of its fundamentals, will be much as it is today despite everything else that may have changed. Only minimal adaptation to evolving environments will have been made.

The futility of specific prediction. Detailed forecasts can go wrong in a much shorter period of time than 25 years—and I have been involved in my share of failed predictions. A case in point is an excellent book, *Campus 1980*, edited by Alvin Eurich and published in 1968. One essay by a most knowledgeable scholar (Sidney Tickton) predicted:

  •"A sharp rise in the number of students enrolled in higher education—sharper than the estimates published by most government agencies." (These estimates, in fact, proved to be too high, beginning in 1969.)

•"A continued upsurge in graduate education." (It shortly became a distressed, if not a disaster, area.)

•"A substantial increase in the number of faculty members and assistants—but not substantial enough to match the increase in enrollments." (Some faculty members are now being let go for lack of enrollments.)

•"Greatly increased spending by institutions of higher learning to meet expanding needs for their services." (The "new depression" in higher education began shortly after this prediction was made.)

•That "salaries and benefits of higher education faculty members will rise substantially over the years." (They have not, in recent years, even kept up with cost of living.)

The Carnegie Commission is another case in point. Commission estimates with regard to enrollments, the number of new institutions, faculty salaries, and the percent of the Gross National Product spent on institutions of higher education, all proved optimistic. The major lesson to be learned is: caution in advance, humility afterwards.

The inherent distortions in today's view of tomorrow. The present provides a prejudiced glimpse of the future; prejudiced, first, by the current mood. In the early and middle sixties, the mood was euphoric—as William W. Marvel wrote in *Campus 1980*, "All trend curves will be up." Today the mood is one of depression. All, or at least many, trend curves are down; gloom is chic. What will the mood be tomorrow?

Prejudiced, too, by current desires. Nevitt Sanford wrote in the Eurich volume that "this whole universe [of students] will have moved, and will be moving, in the direction pointed to by the student activists." Today, the residue of their activism is almost nil and countertrends—vocationalism, for example, instead of social concern—have set in. The predictions of today reflect, in part, the desires of today: for more nontraditional education, or for greater use of the new technology, or for millions of new adults in classrooms, or for the substantial triumph of affirmative action in five years (the latter was the official federal policy that was declared in 1972).

Finally, prejudiced by the recent past, Peter Drucker once wrote that "the higher birthrate which reasserted itself in the early forties now appears to be the normal rate." The "normal rate" of today, in fact, is the lowest in our recorded history and substantially below that of the early 1940s. In the 1930s leading economists had been predicting "permanent stagnation" because of the declining birthrate; instead, after World War II, there was the longest boom period in American history. We are now again predicting a new stagnation or at least steady state, in part, again, because of a declining birthrate. Will it hold true this time? Drucker also spoke of the "short supply" of "trained and educated people" continuing indefinitely into the future. The indefinite future now seems to hold an almost excessive oversupply. Does it really? We have been misled before, and yet the recent past is our best clue.

The moral of this is that we find ourselves in a hall of mirrors with distorted reflections all about us. We should be ready to reject, at least in part, each and every one of them.

A further caution about current predictions, particularly in the United States: We tend, as a nation, to overdo our solutions to problems once we have made up our minds to solve them, thus causing new problems (too few become too many PhDs is one illustration). Instead of predicting that all problems get worse and worse, we would do better to predict solutions—sometimes in overkill amounts—and then go on to predict the problems that these solutions will create, ad infinitum.

The already built-in features of tomorrow's house. Two features are already built into the structure of the first decade of the twenty-first century. First, about 35 to 40 percent of all faculty members will be retiring; this reflects the heavy hiring of the 1960s. Second, more than half of all buildings will be subject to replacement or major remodeling. These two facts give rise to all kinds of possibilities for 2000 or 2010: accelerated hiring of women and minorities; introduction of new programs at an unusually fast rate accompanying the new faculty members; acceptance of new architectural designs; massive application of the best results of accumulated technological developments; and a new incentive for PhD study and, thus, an anticipatory renaissance for graduate divisions.

It will be a decade of movement, more like that of the late 1950s and early 1960s than like anything between now and the end of the century. Higher education is tenured in by its faculty and walled in by its physical plant for the next quarter century. A new period of comparative flexibility and freedom of choice will then arrive. Some of the shackles will drop off the wrists and ankles of presidents and trustees. They can do again what they do best—add. For them, subtraction is a most distressing art. The academic house of 2000-2010 will welcome many new tenants and will be in the process of being substantially rebuilt. This observation leads to some advice for the academic young of today who may wish to become a new generation of building presidents: Wait for 2000; by then, other new aspiring builders will have come along.

The certainty of uncertainties. We cannot know in advance what surprises there may be, but we do know that some essential features affecting higher education in the future are subject to substantial fluctuations:

• The birthrate. It was 30 per 1,000 in 1910; 19 in 1935; 27 in 1947; and 15 in 1973. The birthrate affects the demand for elementary schoolteachers quickly, and the demand for college teachers slowly.

• Rates of return on private investments in higher education, particularly as affected by comparative earnings in the labor market for college-level occupations. Students, particularly advanced students, seem to be quite responsive to changes in these rates of return.

• Lifestyles of youth and adults are subject to wide variations.

• The size of the GNP. Recessions and depressions aside, will its long-run rate of growth slow down? And by how much?

• Public priorities, including higher education in competition with other social needs. The priority for higher education rose in the 1960s and is falling now. What will be its future course?

Any predictions that rely on these important factors should be made within broad ranges of possibilities. We are in a period of substantial discontinuities.

The underlying certainty. There is, as a final observation, the certainty that higher education will be more needed in the future than in the past as a supplier of ever more advanced skills, as a source of ever more complex new ideas, as an entry to an ever more desired higher equality of life for individuals, as a supplier of ever more needed social commentary as a basis for social reform, and as a preserver and enhancer of the ever expanding cultural heritage. In its several important services, it will continue to be, as it has been in the past, a growth sector of society—but almost certainly more in qualitative and less in quantitative terms.

Higher education will be even more essential to American society in the year 2000 and beyond than it is today.

> Plato: When the wheel [of education] has once been set
> in motion, the speed is always increasing....
>
> Vladimir: What do we do now?
> Estragon: Wait.

Unlike waiting for Beckett's Godot, we know that the year 2000 will definitely arrive but, like Godot, what it will look like and whether it will bring more good or more evil nobody can know. We have both curiosity and hope.

II

Trends and Aberrations

Lessening Influence
and the Search for Purpose

Lewis B. Mayhew

S ometime in the late nineteenth century, the characteristic mode of American higher education emerged in the form of a complex, multipurpose, utilitarian institution. While there were hundreds of institutions that did not conform to that mode, its ideology nevertheless pervaded higher education and became the mean toward which all institutions seemed to be moving. Thus from the turn of the twentieth century through to the 1970s, while diversity was valued in the abstract, and while there were many different kinds of institutions, in reality there was a reasonably steady transition of most institutions toward the modal type. Technical institutions and normal schools gradually added elements of the liberal arts and sciences, additional professional fields, graduate work, and, in theory at least, an emphasis on faculty research.

Liberal arts colleges added first professional work in education, then business, then preprofessional programs, and eventually the majority of such colleges added some graduate work, if only through the master's degree. Private junior colleges began to evolve into four-year liberal arts colleges and then followed the same evolutionary pattern as other liberal arts colleges. Public junior colleges, except in states that mandated against such evolution, either added advanced and more varied programs by becoming four-year institutions, or else did so under the guise of evening programs and adult education programs. Even the more recently created experimental and nontraditional types of institutions regressed in similar fashion. The Union for Experimenting

Colleges, for example, originally sought to foster experimentation in a handful of liberal arts colleges. Eventually it began to grow more complex with the creation of graduate programs offered in somewhat nontraditional styles and by so doing became a complex, multipurpose consortium of institutions. So did its ideological parent, Antioch College, which converted from a single-campus, liberal arts college to the complex system embracing undergraduate, graduate, and professional programs. The regression tendency has been and continues to be so powerful that in the absence of major external events forcing a reorganization, institutions of higher education in the year 2000 are likely to be quite similar to the archetypal multipurpose institution existing in 1975. To be sure, some quantitative differences may be detected. Smaller liberal arts colleges, lacking the capacity to evolve, are likely to die; and public institutions are likely to be universally organized into systems of campuses.

Although the evolution of American institutions of higher education toward the modal form has been reasonably steady, there have been a few significant changes that in turn suggest others. However, virtually all of the major changes came about as a result of external and quite unpredictable factors. Since prediction of powerful new social forces is virtually impossible, anticipation of markedly new purposes or practices in higher education is similarly impossible. Consider the increase in size and cost of American higher education during the past 20 years, with enrollments increasing almost tenfold and cost almost threefold. Enrollment increases resulted from the unpredictable upsurge in the birthrate following World War II, from two unexpected wars that made college attendance preferable to military service, to an unexpected period of affluence resulting in part from the World War II-stimulated economy, followed by an economy organized to refurbish war-devastated regions and to help underdeveloped countries solve agricultural, medical, and technological problems. Sustained affluence contributed to rising personal expectations, hence to increasingly more high school graduates convinced that higher education was the pathway to preferment.

A second major change was the attention given by institutions of higher education to segments of the population previously beyond the educational pale. The substantial increase in the numbers of blacks, Chicanos, and Native Americans attending college, especially in the sixties, forced major revisions in curricula, financial aid, and expectations of performance. The demands of minority groups seem, at least in part, to be related to the revolution of colonized peoples all over the world. That revolution was unexpected, and it expanded more rapidly than expected as a result of the dislocations of power and authority in the aftermath of World War II. Of course, some shifts in relationships between colonial powers and their colonies had begun even before World War II (as, for example, the British negotiations with India); but the speed with which the world was swept by the revolutionary spirit was the unpredictable part.

The unpredictability of institutional concern for minority groups is dramatized by the United States' experience. Following the Supreme Court decisions of 1954 regarding segregation, there were changes in the status of blacks in the United States. However, institutions of higher education modified their postures hardly at all with respect to recruiting, admitting, and making special provisions for black students until the death of Martin Luther King. That event stands as a watershed; afterwards, institutional relationships with blacks and other minority students took on new and unexpected forms.

A third major change in American higher education was the sudden preoccupation with research, especially research funded by external agencies. Prior to World War II, a few institutions stressed the primacy of research and some scholars conducted rather impressive studies supported for the most part with their own funds and done during time stolen from the demands of heavy teaching schedules. There was, of course, reasonably large-scale research in agriculture and, to some extent, in medicine and engineering. Further, before World War II institutions were genuinely frightened of taking funds from the federal government on the ground that such a relationship would jeopardize academic freedom. Then came the atomic bomb, radar, and the proximity fuse, all spawned directly by the war. The model of federal and institutional cooperation for research purposes became both visible and viable as a result of postwar affluence, and sponsored research became a hallmark of the distinguished institution—a characteristic that all other institutions sought assiduously. By the 1960s, research seriously threatened the integrity of the older purpose of higher education, namely teaching.

Of a different order were the changes in American higher education brought about through the elimination of barriers to educational opportunity. In 1950, 10 barriers to educational opportunity were identified: economic barriers; barriers of race, religion, and national origin; geographic barriers; curricular and administrative barriers; sexual barriers; social barriers; political and legislative barriers; barriers put up by professional groups; barriers imposed on an individual by the social attitudes, values, and standards of his family; and barriers generated by psychological reaction to a frustrating situation. Most of these remain. Geographic barriers, however, and barriers of religion have been largely removed, while barriers of race and economic condition have been partially removed. It is now possible for the large majority of college-age youth to attend colleges located within commuting distance of their homes. It is also possible for Jews to attend virtually any institution they wish, and for Catholics to attend, without feelings of guilt, any secular institution. But the removal of these barriers seems, for the most part, to be related to the historical accidents of population explosion, unexpected affluence, and the revolt of the colonial peoples. Those barriers that might have been overcome through rational decisions largely persist.

There have, of course, been a number of changes within institutions brought about, at least in part, by internal discussion and decision, yet even these changes seem to behave in erratic and unpredictable ways, thus precluding any simple extrapolation into the future. It should be pointed out that the various practices and processes of higher education seem historically to have shifted periodically from one extreme position to another in an almost pendulumlike manner. All of these positions may be viewed in a 300-year historical context, but they may also be viewed in the shorter period of the twentieth century. Along one continuum collegiate curricula shifted from highly elective in the first third of the century to somewhat prescribed in the second third, back to somewhat freely elective in the last third. Another dimension involves elitism versus egalitarianism. There was something of an egalitarian flavor at the turn of the century as the ideal of land-grant institutions became thoroughly assimilated. This gave way, in part, to an implied elitism in the twenties and thirties when only the well-to-do or wealthy could afford to stay long in college. The period of veteran enrollments after World War II produced a resurgence of egalitarian rhetoric that gave way to elite meritocratic rhetoric after Sputnik. The sixties saw a rising tide of egalitarianism but by the midseventies, elitism has come to the fore again as new postsecondary institutions are created to care for the nonelite. Still another dimension contrasts a theoretical orientation with a real-life orientation—again, practices fluctuate, with institutions emphasizing the academic at one time and real life at another. The seventies came to be characterized by intense emphasis on real-life experiences, but by 1975 abuses accompanying real-life emphases seemed to be producing a reaction. One could go on. During some periods the student is seen as the proper focus for the curriculum, while at others the subject or discipline is so viewed. Sometimes a humanistic ethos seems to prevail, sometimes a scientific.

The unpredictability and asymmetry of these continua are revealed by the fact that the pendulum swings along each continuum are not necessarily coordinated with swings along the others. A real-life curricular emphasis can be accompanied by either an elective or prescribed curriculum. With no perceivable consistency, there can be very little precise prediction.

Presumably, if one knows with some surety the likely future of social, economic, political, or technological courses, one could make some reasonable guesses as to the likely future of higher education. Unfortunately, prediction of such courses is still so primitive that the chances of error are considerably greater than the chances for correct prediction. Who could have predicted that a small police action in Southeast Asia would help force two Presidents out of office? Who could have predicted that in less than 30 years the creation of a small Jewish state would produce one of the most massive redistributions of wealth in history? Who could have predicted that the major antagonists in World War II, which was ostensibly fought over radically different ideologies, would in less than a third of a century become an almost solid block of democratic, capitalistic nations?

Yet there may be a few matters that can be anticipated—at least in the United States. First, it would seem likely that the historic trend of a steadily decreasing birthrate will continue and that the somewhat erratic upsurge in the birthrate after World War II will not be repeated. It also seems likely that the nation will enter a sustained period of stabilized economic growth, if for no other reason than the diminishing of natural resources needed to sustain rapid economic growth. Given a more stable economic growth, it also seems likely that technological research and development are bound to stabilize. While there could very well be some minor fluctuations in the next 25 years with respect to each of these three, the overall trends seem reasonably clear.

The bases for prediction in higher education are thin and tenuous, but perhaps several possibilities can be singled out. The first concerns whether the remainder of the twentieth century will see a revolution in higher education comparable to that which occurred between approximately 1870 and 1910. During those 40 years recitation gave way to the lecture and seminar; generalist instructors gave way to highly professional specialists; a small, humanistically oriented core of prescribed courses was replaced by a steadily proliferating number of specialized courses available for free election on the part of students; the library and laboratory became essential resources; departments were created and much of professional education was given the form that has lasted until the present. There is some speculation that in view of intense experimentation and attempted innovation during the sixties and seventies, higher education may be on the verge of a second radical shift. However, this does not appear likely, unless higher education assumes, with public support, some major new purpose to which innovations and experimentation can make a substantial contribution.

What seems to have happened during this earlier period was that higher education assumed the two additional functions of research and service in addition to its traditional one of education, especially education for character development. Those two new purposes were admirably served by such innovations as the department and a free elective system, and in aggregate the innovations coalesced around the new purposes. The question is, What are the chances that some new purpose for all of higher education may be evolving? A number of new purposes have been espoused, such as the college and university campus assuming a redemptive function, becoming a model for democratic community living, becoming a clinic, or, even in truth, becoming a secular church. None of these seems likely to muster the requisite social, political, and economic support to enter the mainstream of higher education. In the absence of a new purpose, then, it can be predicted that the processes of higher education in the year 2000 will not be appreciably different from those in the 1970s. To make the point further, consider this description: "Bachelor's degree requirements were for 120 hours, 45 of which had to be distributed between the broad divisions of natural science, social science, and humanities. Courses were taught through a pattern of large lectures and smaller discussions, with laboratories attached for relevant subjects. Courses were offered by individual departments with a sequence of courses designed primarily to prepare students for future graduate work and with only passing attention to the needs of the nonspecialist. Classes were scheduled at regular intervals with an hour of class conduct being generally worth a semester hour of academic credit (of course, the one-to-one credit did not obtain for science laboratories). Two years of foreign language were required but increasingly ways have been found to circumvent the requirement. Students typically studied intensively at mid term and final examination time and less assiduously during the remainder of the semester. Registration required three days at the beginning of the fall semester and one and a half to two days at the beginning of the spring semester. Some courses scheduled field trips and other courses tried to involve students in semi-independent research."

The academic program thus described was that in effect at the University of Illinois in the early 1930s. It is for the most part still in effect in the 1970s, with a few minor exceptions such as the use of a throat microphone by lecturers and the use of the computer by some students in some experimental classes. In the absence of some major new purpose, that description very likely will be applicable 25 years from now.

The form, processes, and practices of higher education are likely to remain the same. However, it does seem plausible to predict that higher education in the not too distant future will be less influential in the life of society than it was during the 1960s. During that decade many viewed higher education as a principal instrument for the achievement of a wide variety of social needs. Actual performance revealed an inability of collegiate institutions to solve such problems as unemployment, the degrading conditions in the inner city, or the inequitable distribution of wealth. That is not to say that higher education was without achievement, but that expectations of what it could accomplish were exalted out of all sense of reality. The seventies seem to have ushered in a period of less grandiose expectations, accompanied, of course, by less influence. Independent research institutes seem much more likely now to become the major research centers, and apprenticeships and work-service activities seem more efficient as far as easing large numbers of the young into adulthood.

As the number of people receiving college degrees has increased, the value of that degree as a passport to preferment has diminished. This does not mean that there will not be screening for the limited number of "good jobs," but rather that the screening will make use of other techniques or attributes. It is even possible that parental status may once again be a recognized determinant.

Throughout much of the history of American higher education a major purpose has been a custodial one, with institutions caring for late adolescents until the labor market or marriage was ready to receive and make use of them. Many of the practices of higher education, including the wide range of student personnel services, were designed to fulfill this custodial role and institutions did think of themselves as appropriate custodians. Given the reduction in the age of adulthood and the new alternative lifestyle of students, and given the increase in the discontinuities that characterize college attendance, it seems likely that the custodial role must inevitably diminish. With such a reduction, especially as commuting students come to predominate, it is then logical to expect a reduction in such services as the health center, counseling clinic, campus dining rooms, and elaborate programs of recreation.

Of a different order is the role played by private higher education. The United States is one of the few nations that has historically employed both publicly controlled and privately controlled
higher education. From the end of World War II onward there has
been a steady decline in the proportion of students being served by
the private sector. There are and have been attempts to arrest this
decline but none has had more than momentary success. In the absence of powerful new purposes and sources of support, it seems
likely that the private sector will continue to decline to a point
where it will educate perhaps 10 to 15 percent of the cohort group,
with these numbers being almost equally divided between those
attending the few elite universities and those attending lesser institutions because of the amenities the private sector provides.

However, it is still possible to visualize a different future if
American higher education should assume, with support, some
major new mission or purpose. Of the competing purposes the one
most likely to gain recognition and support would be a social meliorist purpose. Such a purpose represents a qualitatively different
extension of the older service mission. The social meliorist institution would offer educational activities to all groups that wanted
them—wherever and whenever. The social meliorist institution
would include many programs to rectify the educational and
cultural deficiencies of many different groups of people. Such institutions might well become the largest patrons of the arts as well
as the operators of legal-aid services, storefront medical centers,
day-care centers, and educational programs to meet every expressed need. Present strategies of finance, of course, will not
allow the social meliorist role, nor is society yet ready to recognize
the legitimacy of collegiate institutions in undertaking such activities. But this could change, and if it did then it seems likely that
some of the more promising educational innovations might find
their way into mainline practices.

At least three major processes would then become central. The
first of these is the computer adapted to educational purposes with
computer terminals available in many homes. The second would
be videotape recordings, particularly videotape casettes, which
could carry the richness of the campus to the farthest reaches of a
state. The third would be much greater acceptance of reasonably
precisely measured life experiences as part of formal programs of
study. Each of these three has limited use in traditional programs,
but they seem to be ideally suited to a broader range of services
institutions might render under the banner of social meliorism.

On the Road
to a Learning Society

Arthur M. Cohen

In a felicitous essay in *The Lives of a Cell*, Lewis Thomas defines three levels of technology in medicine. One, he says, is a large body of "nontechnology" to comfort patients who have diseases that are not under control. Here, a large part of the doctor's time is spent providing reassurance or merely standing by. At the next level is a kind of halfway technology designed to make up for disease or to postpone death. Organ transplants fall into that category as does the management of heart disease. This level requires a continuing expansion of hospital facilities and highly trained people. We do not know how to prevent the diseases that lead to the disabilities but we do know how to mitigate their effects. Thomas's third level of technology leads to genuinely decisive action, exemplified by immunization against diseases that once killed or crippled large sections of the population. The price for preventive medicine is exceedingly modest in comparison with the cost of attenuating disease or of just standing by, but prevention rests on large-scale research efforts to isolate causes.

Education is not medicine but parallels can be drawn. Education is a technology with a corps of professional people ministering to clients. And as physicians argue over what constitutes good health, so educators question definitions of the educated person. Professional educators spend practically all their time practicing at stages one and two of Thomas's technology. A sizable effort is expended on caring for clients for whom nothing much is or can be done. Call it standing by, caring for, or maintaining custody over, it is a major function at all levels of schooling. Another large effort goes into remedying defects occasioned by earlier neglect. Every type and level of school has programs to teach what was supposed to have been learned earlier. As for the third level of technology, educational research is not about to discover a serum, a philosopher's stone that can turn the base metal of the populace into the gold of learned scholars. Research and development expenditures in higher education are modest at best and most of them are spent on redesigning patterns of college organization rather than on research toward better ways of effecting learning. Any change in enhancing individual learning capability in the next generation will come about through brain research; but neither a chemical compound nor genetic modification is on the horizon. We cannot expect immunization against ignorance in the near future. We can only anticipate more of the same in education—people learning on their own, with and without the intervention of schools and colleges.

Nonetheless, several basic structural changes in higher education are imminent. Until recently, patterns of schooling began with the elementary school close to one's home, progressed through a middle school somewhat farther away, and then to a secondary school to which one may have had to ride a bus. To continue studies after high school one usually went to a distant college. Each institution was progressively larger, farther, and more selective. College was the culmination, the sacred precinct where the individual was housed, transformed, and then returned to his community or to the larger world.

This sequence is being transformed. Increasingly, postsecondary education takes place closer to home. Admissions requirements diminish; travel obligations and costs subside. There is a greater variety of opportunity for continuing education within everyone's commuting range than ever before. People start and stop their postsecondary education repeatedly. Moreover, various types of colleges flourish in every city of size. Many states have low-cost colleges within reasonable commuting distance of 95 percent of the population, and the trend is toward even greater diffusion of opportunity. Most publicly supported colleges are expanding their course offerings away from the main campus. Thus the pattern of education as occurring in progressively more distant locales is being reversed. In the off-campus centers, people study in association with their neighbors, just as they went to elementary school with children living in their own vicinity. The age-graded campus enclaves are diminishing in relative size.

By the year 2000, most colleges—especially those in urban areas—will look like combinations of today's university extension centers, occupational training schools, and adult basic education centers, coupled with the existing campus forms. (The two-year community colleges have already moved far along this path.) Each will have a central campus and several satellite centers and, in addition, will offer courses in single locations. All types of media will be employed, including newspaper courses, televised lessons, and a variety of reproducible materials. Many will effect liaisons with local cultural enterprises and seek to enhance aesthetic awareness through design, recitals, and continuing exhibitions. Thus the colleges will spread through their communities.

Even now, some colleges store and display instructional video cassettes through the facilities of their local public libraries. This allows for demand use—videotaped instruction where anyone can see any program at any time—and exemplifies a further shift toward the localized and the immediate. One can see a person at the turn of the millennium interacting with his fellows in a class at a satellite center, viewing a video cassette to learn something else, and attending a campus for a special event for yet another part of his education. He receives varied educational presentations at his own pace, in his own city, on his own terms.

The move toward a potpourri of educational offerings presents perceptual problems. A campus has bounds; it looks like a college. But an institution that offers courses in church basements and recreation centers is unfamiliar. Who or what is one's alma mater when one has taken nearly all of one's classes in office buildings at night? Where does one go for Homecoming?

The definition of "student" is also changing, and current categories may not be appropriate to describe the college populations of the next century. A student today is defined by an institution as one who is on its roll book. But the number and percent of people who both work and go to school part time is steadily increasing. We are moving more toward a dual definition: institutionally mandated status, and the status of a person enrolled in a course or two at a local college who sees himself not as a student but in terms of his profession. Further, many colleges offer concerts for credit if the attendees enroll in a music appreciation course, open their swimming pool to the public for physical education credit, and present lectures for credit in political science. When they call people "students" for participating in these types of activities, and give credit by examination and credit for experience, there is no limit to the number who may be so designated. Accordingly, we will see single colleges enrolling as much as 30 to 40 percent of their district's population. The distinctions among students, nonstudents, and former students will be artificial and useless.

Satellite centers and other off-campus classrooms present perceptual problems for the college staff as well. Traditionally, many faculty have shunned the off-campus class because it changes their patterns of interaction with students and colleagues. The instructor's role shifts when he becomes a circuit rider. He must create an entire learning environment at off-hours in a building that has other primary uses. He is recruited, selected, and evaluated by an administrative functionary rather than by his peers. The concepts of academic departments and faculty perquisites also change. New images of the educator emerge.

These structural modifications will be accompanied by certain changes in our perceptions of human understanding. Heretofore knowledge has been viewed as though it were finite, as though it were a property in a zero-sum game. Young people are told, "Go to school and you will earn more than your fellows. You will move ahead in social standing." Normative testing and grading are built on this assumption of relative individual worth. Knowledge is being marketed as though there were only so much to go around. If one has it he has something that no one else can possess. But this view proceeds from a fundamental error about the nature of knowledge and from an unproved view of innate human variability.

By the year 2000 we will understand that knowledge is a pattern of interrelationships among people and information. It should not be put into the category of a staple economic good; when it is construed as a form of wealth similar to energy or land, it is debased. It differs in kind from property because one person's possessing it does not diminish the knowledge of another. On the contrary, if one knows and another does not, both are the lesser for it. When one person gains knowledge, the holdings of all are increased proportionately. The more people there are who understand, the better the community. The community as a society of people in the business of gaining knowledge will be more nearly the operating view.

Still, a move away from the productivity model that assesses educational institutions on the number of students who flow through them will not come easily. The United States is, and will continue to be, a credential society. Institutions that sanction learning by awarding degrees and certificates will still be with us. The difference is that there will be room under the higher education rubric for more broadly defined learning centers than exist today.

A major force propelling society toward this changed view is issuing—inadvertently to be sure—from the faculty themselves.

Currently, faculty moves toward a greater measure of control over the conditions of their work are resulting in higher salaries and a more precise definition of their tasks. Yet every contract that spells out class size and faculty-student ratio mandates a continuation of education's high labor-intensive character. Since wages are increasing in the face of a stable ratio of students to staff, productivity in effect is decreasing. As a result, education demands an ever-increasing proportion of funds.

But this trend cannot continue indefinitely. Instead, faculty members at some institutions will accept the technologies, aides, and paraprofessional assistants that allow them to teach more students, thus increasing their productivity. The teacher as autonomous manager—the director of a corps of aides—is already well advanced in some fields, notably in the biological sciences and the occupational skills area. We have also seen the development of well-integrated instructional resource centers that assist instructors in becoming producers of reproducible media. By the year 2000 some instructor-managers will be highly paid professional people earning today's equivalent of $35,000 a year, assisted by relatively low-paid technicians and apprentices, responsible for managing the learning experiences of hundreds of students. Those who shun this—and there are many, opting for the one-teacher-25-students-in-a-classroom model—will be forced to fight continually for a greater share of public funds.

Another type of instructional situation is developing even more rapidly. Here the hourly-rate instructor, or "adjunct" professor, to whom the institution has no commitment beyond the span of a single term, is the norm, especially in those colleges that are heavily committed to community services and lifelong learning. (The university extension centers offer a model for this.) In the majority of cases these instructors work also at other jobs, teaching only because of interest in the field and the desire to earn a salary supplement. In this regard they resemble the part-time students who pursue other activities and attend a class or two in their area of interest, either for upgrading in their vocation or for their own enlightenment. In the community colleges even now, half the faculty is part time. This accelerating pattern points toward a coalition of full-time program heads, division chairpersons, and nonacademic personnel as managers of a corps of transient teachers. The learning society will still be institutionally based but the processes of learning and working will come closer together both for teacher and student.

This picture of the instructor of the future is based on the assumption that certain contemporary concerns are transient. The current emphasis on attempting to define better criteria for faculty evaluation, for example, will soon pass its peak. Staff evaluation will take the form it has always had; the faculty member who can keep his students enrolled and interested will be suitably rewarded. And the emerging phenomenon of faculty members requesting separate pay for tasks such as advising students and serving on college committees will fall of its own weight.

By the year 2000 we will have recognized too that in education we need not choose between excellence and equality. We can have both. Guns-and-butter dilemmas need be posed only when resources are finite. Knowledge is infinite. Some types of colleges must and should cost more than others. The major research institutions, offering prestige along with their degrees, will stand on a base of community colleges and public and private four-year institutions. All will coexist.

The long-term problems in higher education are not funding or patterns of organization. They do not concern who decides what shall be offered or whether power resides locally or at the state or national level. Education is infinitely broad; no one system, no one medium, no one type of school solves all community education needs. Variation in form is necessary. The image of the learning community precludes no medium or organizational pattern.

Many functions must be advanced. Higher education must offer a place where people can maintain themselves in socially sanctioned activities. It must serve the higher learning. It must offer certification for those who need passports to better jobs even though an exclusive view of higher education as manpower training is self-defeating. Nor is education for leisure time its major purpose; education is becoming a leisure-time activity of itself. Higher education must serve all these purposes while itself acting as an agent of coalescence between specific learning and general enlightenment, between a variety of forms of publicly available media.

The educational equivalent of administering inoculations against communicable diseases will not be found. However, a different analogy with medical technologies may be useful. Major advances in health come when certain environmental modifications are made—when sewers are put underground, water is fluoridated, clean air and industrial safety standards are adopted. In short, many of the most significant contributions to human health have taken place outside hospitals. Educators would do well to consider that the most significant advances in higher education could occur outside the colleges.

A Clash of Tangled Forces

Alan Pifer

As a result of its transformation in recent decades from a privileged activity of the few to a democratic expectation of the many, higher education cannot today be viewed as an autonomous, self-directed enterprise apart from the society at large. It must be seen as an integral facet of the general order, moving along with it and reflecting it. I do not see this situation changing over the next 25 years. There may—I hope, will—be protected, truly independent enclaves within higher education that will move in their own direction and at their own pace, but, in the main, higher education will march in step with the major trends of the nation at large. This is not to say that our colleges and universities will not have some influence on the tempo and course of that march. Of course they will. But, reciprocally, they will be heavily influenced by it.

To make predictions about the future of higher education, therefore, is to speculate about the principal economic, social, and political trends that will be affecting the nation generally in the future. Beyond this formidable difficulty is the problem of disengaging one's predictions about what will happen from what one would like to have happen. The most one can do is to suggest a few major trends that it seems probable, or at least possible, will give shape to our national life in the future, and to indicate how these trends may affect higher education.

First, it seems probable to me that the nation will continue its long, tortoiselike journey toward equality of rights and opportunity for all its citizens, irrespective of race, sex, cultural background, or economic station. While there will be intervals of no progress and even of regression, I do not believe we will renege on our historic commitment to a just society. Neither do I believe the nation will have completed this journey by the year 2000. It is thus safe to predict that our colleges and universities will still be coping in various ways with the problems produced by gross disparities in income distribution, unequal schooling, segregated housing, and other manifestations of injustice and inequality.

I would hope that within higher education substantial progress toward full equality of opportunity will have been made and that the need for affirmative action programs will all but have disappeared. By that time, certainly, the older white males who now dominate higher education, some of whom retain deep-seated convictions about the incapacity of women and minorities to attain the highest level of scholarship and administration, will have passed out of the system. Furthermore, the supply of highly qualified women and minorities available for tenured academic posts and senior administrative positions will be very much larger than it is today. One must not, of course, assume that all this will just happen naturally. Continued effort and considerable pressure will also be necessary.

As the work of the Carnegie Council on Policy Studies in Higher Education shows so clearly, enrollments in the 1980s and 1990s will be heavily influenced by the decisions the nation makes with respect to the funding of open access to higher education. If this funding is meager and inadequate, as at present, many able young people will not be able to go to college. If it is generous, the impact on enrollments, and therefore also on the general financial stability of higher educational institutions, will be substantial. The symbiotic relationship between external public policy decisions and what happens internally in higher education is well illustrated in this regard.

A second force that will without doubt be even more prominent in American life at the end of the century than it is today will be the pressure to develop new technology through which the nation can maintain its high standard of living despite the disappearance of the cheap raw materials on which it has depended so heavily. Possibly by then new energy sources to supplement and even replace oil will have become practical, but the need to improve efficiency in the use of all kinds of resources and to develop many new ones will be general and relentless.

It seems almost certain, therefore, that the national demand for technology, and the accompanying requirement for a pure and applied science base to sustain it, will be considerably greater at the end of the coming quarter century than it has been even in recent decades. This demand cannot help but have a heavy impact on higher education, both in its research capacity and in the production of highly trained men and women. I see no prospect of our colleges and universitie's being bypassed in the intensifying struggle that lies ahead to maintain a high national standard of living in the face of difficulties that will dwarf anything we have yet experienced.

A third major trend we can predict fairly confidently because it is already well under way is a change in the prevailing American concept of how a "decent standard of living" should be defined. As I have suggested, there will be no letup in the quest for economic well-being, but material welfare alone will not be considered sufficient by most people. As population pressure grows and more and more people live in physically restricted environments, there will be an even greater concern for individual, humanistic self-fulfillment. This will be expressed in a quest for more spiritually meaningful experiences, for greater access to open space and to nature, and for more satisfying forms of recreation—including learning for the sake of learning rather than for simple vocational advancement.

This movement, of course, will create pressures for forms of public expenditure, on parks and the arts, for example, that will compete with the pressure for expenditure on higher education. But it will also, in my view, greatly enlarge the demand for part-time study by adults and consequently serve to broaden the base of support for higher educational expenditure. Some skeptics believe this alleged demand for adult recreational learning opportunities has been greatly oversold and will never materialize. Americans, they say, will be as glued to their television sets in the future as they are today. I disagree. I believe there is already a great, unsatisfied yearning for serious study by adults, and this will become even greater as we advance toward the end of the century. What obscures the demand now is a combination of high cost and inconvenience to the consumer in delivery of the product. As higher educational institutions find ways to reduce prices or to receive more generous tax support to subsidize the consumer, and as they move toward much greater flexibility of location and hour in meeting adult requirements, I firmly believe the existence of a substantial demand will be fully evident.

Growing concern for the quality of life will, it seems to me, produce not only an increased demand for opportunities for adult learning but also, within higher education, a strong revival of interest in the liberal arts. Of particular interest will be those fields that have most to say about the ideas, emotions, instincts, spiritual yearnings, moral sensitivities, and aesthetic sensibilities that have animated men and women throughout the ages. This revival will be further stimulated, I believe, by widespread disillusionment, on the part of many of those who attended college in the midseventies, with the excessively vocational nature of their experience. Reacting then to the narrow, stultifying training they had earlier sought out of panic, they will be looking for a broader, deeper, and more satisfying educational experience that will give them not only wider horizons and greater career choice but increased understanding of themselves and the world and of their place in it.

A fourth trend that may well develop in the remaining years of this century will be a growing public concern for the welfare of all post-high-school-age youth, and new public policies to meet the needs of this group. Currently disregarded, even seemingly disliked, by the society at large, these young people are in the anomalous position of being, in effect, an unneeded, unwanted, superfluous element of the population. With only the most limited opportunity for employment, much of it of a dead-end nature, they have had the choice of entering higher education, enlisting in the military, or doing nothing, the last of these frequently leading to another option—getting into trouble. Given these alternatives, it is no wonder that these people and their parents have seen higher education as the most constructive choice available. Indeed, as an alternative to getting into trouble, with the heavy and often continuing costs to society it entails, public support of higher education has in actuality been not a burden on the taxpayer but a considerable bargain.

It seems possible to me that recognition may grow of the critical importance of the transitional years from youth to adulthood and the nation may begin to ask how all young people might have a constructive experience during this period, with a view to helping them become functioning, contributing members of society for the balance of their lives, rather than a costly drag on it. Preventive investment in youth, rather than costly programs to deal with adult wreckage, would seem to be a sensible approach, and perhaps it will come, although there is little in the nation's present public policy to suggest that it will.

Nevertheless, if it does, the effect on higher education could be considerable. At the most general level, the very large sum of money that would be needed to support activities that enrolled all youth might, at least in part, have to be found by taking funds away from higher education, since the savings accruing from reduced adult wreckage would not be fully realized for some time to come.

On the face of it, this would be a disaster for higher education. It would not only mean less money for the colleges and universities, but if the new kinds of programs and institutions that were developed to cater to youth training, socialization, and maturation were so attractive to young people generally and to their parents that large numbers were diverted away from higher education, it could mean a sharp drop in enrollments. In the end, however, the advantages to the nation might be considerable because it would permit the colleges and universities to concentrate their attention on the abler students doing true college-level work, as well as to devote more attention to adults. Some institutions would, of course, be unable to survive in these new circumstances and would have to close, which in some cases would represent a real loss to the society.

Alternatively, of course, the new youth provision might be developed within higher education by an enormous expansion of its community college sector and a transformation of this institution into something that better served the full range of youth needs. One could perhaps envisage the community college becoming a place that provided not only training but also induction into the world of work, comprehensive youth counseling and, most important of all, the means for young people to initiate and take responsibility for operating a wide range of volunteer service programs. The notion that community colleges should begin to move in that direction, without abandoning any of their present functions, is intriguing, although the argument could also be made that this new purpose would never be served well by these institutions because of competition from existing purposes.

A final major trend that I think will be increasingly apparent during the remainder of this century will be an ever lengthening list of public needs for which the American people will consider government responsible. There will, of course, be much rhetoric against big government and perhaps some real attempts to reduce its responsibilities; but the general trend, whether we like it or not, will be in the other direction.

This steady enlargement of governmental responsibility will in some cases increase the importance of higher education to the nation as, for example, in meeting the expanded need for health care personnel that will follow the passage of national health insurance legislation. But the trend will also increase competition for the tax dollar. As a result, I see growing social pressure ahead, pressure that will be irresistible, for substantial reductions in the costs of higher education. Since these reductions will in time be forced on higher education willy-nilly by public officials, it will behoove higher educational institutions themselves to undertake some substantial experiments in major cost cutting right now, with a view to finding out how this may be done with the least damage to quality.

Among the possibilities for substantial savings to the taxpayer and the consumer, although not to institutions, will be experiments in reducing the total length of the educational process. Some of these experiments should include secondary education as well as higher education to find out if, for some students at any rate, it is not possible by means of better coordination between the two levels to reduce the combined time span by at least a year. Some experiments along these lines are already under way and others should be mounted. The ultimate viability of major cost cutting via this route will, of course, rest on evidence that the graduate is not only as well educated, perhaps better, but is every bit as employable or as admissible to postbaccalaureate work as someone with the additional year to his or her credit.

These five major social trends—the continued quest for social justice, the unabated demand for new technology, the search for an improved quality of life, a new societal concern for all youth, and increasing pressure on the tax dollar—are only a few of the possible forces in the larger society that may radically affect higher education by the year 2000. A longer list would, for example, certainly include the impact of events and movements on the international scene.

Even taking just these five trends, it is extremely difficult to predict what their net effect will be. Will the incompatibilities and contradictions among these forces and others make higher education a more or less central institution? My guess is the former. On balance, the evidence suggests to me that, far from the decline in its significance some observers predict, the most likely outcome will be just the opposite. While substantial changes will no doubt take place in the enterprise by the end of the century, I have little doubt that at that time higher education will be perceived to be at least as important to the nation as it is considered to be today, and probably a good deal more so.

Money and Other Trifles

John D. Millett

Colleges and universities as discrete and separate enterprises confront some very troublesome financial circumstances over the next decade or two. To some extent it may be said that higher education as a social institution has never had a period of time when the financing of the endeavor did not experience difficulty. The sources of financial support for any individual college or university are threefold: charges to students, subventions of governments, and the beneficence of philanthropy. At all times in American history, these varied sources of income have had a differential impact for different colleges and universities, but they have seldom provided all the support that the individual enterprises thought they needed or deserved.

In the 30 years after World War II it is fair to say that institutions of higher education underwent a substantial change in their economic status. This change may be described as one from genteel poverty to modest affluence. The total current operating income available to institutions of higher education in 1950 was about $2.3 billion, and in 1974 current operating income was around $30.5 billion. This was a thirteenfold increase; the corresponding enrollment increase, however, was only around fourfold, and the consumer price index merely doubled in this same period of time. Thus in terms of dollars of constant purchasing power and in terms of enrollment expansion, institutions of higher education might have expected in 1974 to have had an income of some $18 billion. Instead, institutions had an income of over $30 billion.

A good part of this increase in income represented an expansion in the scope of activities performed by institutions of higher education: an increase in enrollment in graduate and graduate professional programs, a considerable expansion of sponsored research, an expansion of student aid, an increase in sponsored public service projects, and an increase in auxiliary enterprises (especially the housing and feeding of students). But a substantial part of the increase in income represented higher tuition prices charged to students and a considerable increase in state government support of instructional activity, especially faculty salaries.

In spite of the increase in income from $2.3 billion in 1950 to nearly $25 billion by 1971, the pattern of expenditures by institutions of higher education remained relatively stable in this period of time. About four fifths of all expenditures were for educational and general activities as these were defined in 1974. Only about 20 percent were for auxiliary enterprises, hospitals, and independent operations. Within the broad category of educational and general activities, the distribution of expenditures was also quite comparable in the two time periods of 1950 and 1971. There was some increase in the proportion of institutional resources spent for student aid, and some decline in the percentage spent for operation and maintenance of the capital plant. This last circumstance resulted from the relative newness of at least half of all academic buildings by 1971. Within the category of auxiliary enterprises, hospitals, and independent operations, there was a considerable shift in the proportion of expenditures for these activities. This change reflected the expansion of medical education and of teaching hospitals as well as the higher costs of operating hospital facilities. Furthermore, the federal government substantially expanded the number and scope of specialized research facilities operated under contract by certain universities.

Within the grouping of educational and general activities, 70 to 73 percent of all expenditures in both years went for the support of so-called "primary" programs: instruction, research, public service, and student aid. Only 30 percent in 1950 and 27 percent in 1971 of institutional expenditures went into support programs, or "overhead."

When we turn to the pattern of income for the two years of 1950 and 1971, the comparison is somewhat different from that for expenditures. First of all, income derived from sales and services of auxiliary enterprises, hospitals, and independent operations declined in relation to educational and general income. In 1950, income from auxiliary enterprises was considerably in excess of expenditures for these activities, partly because of the large number of temporary facilities being operated and partly because of the desire to accumulate some capital with which to build new facilities.

Within the category of educational and general income, there was a considerable increase in the proportion derived from state government and a decline in that from the federal government. This decline largely reflected a change in the handling of educational benefits for veterans between World War II and the end of the Korean War. After World War II the federal government paid veterans' benefits directly to the institution in which the veteran was enrolled. After the Korean War educational benefits to veterans were paid directly to the veteran and the veteran student paid his or her tuition directly to the institution.

It is noteworthy that in 1950 and in 1971 only about one fourth of all educational and general income was derived from charges to students. In 1950 the charges of independent colleges and universities had not yet begun the precipitate increase of the 1960s, and in 1971 some 70 percent of all students were enrolled in public institutions of higher education compared with only some 50 percent in 1950.

These data clearly indicate that for higher education institutions as a whole, nearly three fourths of all educational and general income was obtained from governments and from philanthropy. There are other data that indicate that in terms of total income, about 55 percent comes from governments, about 33 percent comes from charges to students, about 4 percent comes from private philanthropy, and about 7 percent comes from miscellaneous sources.

To be sure, the data cited here represent all institutions of higher education, public and independent, large and small, urban and nonurban, complex and relatively simple in purpose and scope. If these data were disaggregated for different kinds of institutions, the proportionate distribution of expenditures and income would reveal considerable diversity.

Nonetheless, this generalized portrait for all institutions of higher education suggests some important factors bearing upon the future. In a period of great expansion in enrollment and in dollars expended, institutions of higher education preserved a generally consistent pattern of expenditures, especially within the category of activities described as educational and general in nature. And insofar as income to finance these activities was concerned, governments remained the primary source of support, while charges to students provided only about one quarter of educational and general income, and philanthropy and other income provided about 14 percent of available support.

The current question of course is that of the probable future alterations in both the pattern of expenditures and the pattern of income. Will institutions of higher education 10 or 25 years from now display much the same kind of expenditure and income pattern as they did in 1950 and in 1971? An even more vexing question is whether real income is likely to be 40 percent greater in the year 2000 than in the year 1975, as it was in 1975 compared with 1950.

In general, it seems very likely that the real income of institutions of higher education will be no greater in the year 2000 than in the year 1975. Indeed, a major concern for institutions of higher education in the remainder of the 1970s and the 1980s is whether or not they will be able to maintain a real income comparable to that obtained in 1970 or in 1975.

The total volume of income received by institutions of higher education may well decline under two circumstances. If the number of full-time equivalent students declines, then state and local government support may decline somewhat and student tuition income may decline. If federal government support for research and public service projects should decline, and if federal government support of education in the health professions should decline, then the total income of institutions of higher education will decline. There is the further prospect that if federal and other support of students through institutions of higher education should decline, then total income will decline.

Obviously, institutions of higher education will at least seek to ensure sufficient increased income to offset rising price levels. The prospect of increased income per unit of service rendered is not very promising as of 1975.

Insofar as the pattern of income is concerned, some changes must be anticipated in the next 25 years. The tuition charges to students will respond to three concerns or policy choices. First, federal programs in support of students may or may not stimulate some increase in tuition charges, especially at public institutions. Second, state governments may encourage public institutions to increase their tuition charges, while offsetting these increases by direct financial assistance to students from lower-income families. And third, both public and independent institutions may well decide to reexamine tuition pricing, and there may be some differential pricing in response to variations in instructional costs. There may be some effort to reduce instructional costs in an effort to stabilize tuition pricing. Any or all of these kinds of change could affect the amount and the proportion of educational and general income derived from student tuition.

There is also the possibility that institutions of higher education may alter the relative scope of some of their activities during the next 25 years. For example, the volume of instruction for course credit in fulfillment of degree requirements might decline, with a corresponding decline in tuition income. On the other hand, faculties might expand substantially their noncredit continuing education activity. On the expenditure side such activity would be classified as public service, and on the income side the charges to participants in these workshops and lectures would be classified as sales and services of educational departments. If there were any sizable alteration in the scope of these kinds of activities, the income pattern of colleges and universities could be substantially changed.

When we turn to the expenditure pattern of institutions of higher education, the relative proportions of expenditures for instruction and public service would be altered by the kind of shift in activities just mentioned. Among the four primary programs of instruction, research, public service, and student aid, some changes are to be expected.

It seems unlikely that university research will be diminished, but it does seem probable that more and more sponsored research will be directed toward particular national needs, such as protection of the environment, conservation and reuse of raw materials, conservation and development of energy resources, economic growth and family economic welfare in relation to environmental protection and productive resources, technological advance in the delivery of services, manpower resources and employment in relation to individual and family welfare, improvements in educational services, and similar kinds of problems.

It seems unlikely that public service activities will decline in the next 25 years, although it is quite possible that less of this activity may be supported by governments and more of the activity may be paid for by charges to those who enroll in or take advantage of the services provided. If there should be more leisure time available to professional and managerial personnel as well as to blue-collar laborers, it is possible that some part of this leisure may be spent in continuing education. It is also becoming apparent that professional licensure may be changed from lifelong validity to time-limited validity. If this does occur, universities will no doubt be involved in the continuing education activity oriented to qualification for renewal of licensure or recertification of professional or paraprofessional competence. Here is another possible expansion of public service activity.

Insofar as instruction is concerned, expenditure volume may change with program change, enrollment change, and cost change. It seems likely that program change will be in the direction of increased enrollments in career, baccalaureate professional, and graduate professional programs, with some corresponding decline in baccalaureate and graduate programs in the arts and sciences. These program and enrollment changes will have an impact upon program costs. Lowered enrollments in some programs will increase student credit hour or per-student costs. Increased enrollments in professional programs could reduce per-student costs, except that there will be pressure to maintain existing costs. Costs could be altered also by changes in instructional procedures or technology. Much will depend upon faculty attitudes and the future course of faculty collective bargaining.

Institutional expenditures for student aid will be influenced by governmental policies and programs, as well as by institutional concerns with the promotion of educational justice. If federal and state governments increasingly provide student aid grants directly to students rather than through institutions, then the institutional accounts will show a reduction both in governmental grant income and in student aid expenditures. Moreover, institutions will continue to have to decide just how much general income derived from student tuition, unrestricted endowment income, and unrestricted gift income will be spent on the promotion of access to their instructional programs.

A major financial concern in the future will be the distribution of educational and general expenditures between primary programs and support programs (academic support, student services, plant operation, and institutional support). A 70-30 relationship will be very difficult if not impossible for institutions to maintain in the next 25 years. Much higher energy costs will increase the expense of plant operation. As academic structures built in the 1960s become older, maintenance costs will rise. Unless student services are reduced, these expenses will increase, especially the expenses of a student health service. Academic support costs may increase with the higher costs of books and periodicals, with greater instructional use of the computer, and with greater use of technological devices of instruction. Institutional support costs will rise as a result of federally imposed requirements relating to affirmative action, unemployment compensation, workmen's compensation, and occupational health and safety.

It has long been recognized that support costs tend to be higher when the institution tends to be smaller. It is not unusual as of 1975 to find independent baccalaureate colleges of under 2,500 full-time students where support programs require 40 or even 45 percent of the educational and general budget. In larger institutions with a very modest number of sponsored research projects, support programs may amount to 35 percent of educational and general expenditure. Only as the number of students enrolled for instruction and as the scope of other activities increase will it be possible to maintain the cost of support programs at less than 35 percent of educational and general expense.

The prospect is that the support costs of institutions of higher education will rise more rapidly than the costs of primary programs. Many of these support costs are externally imposed and can't be controlled by the institutions themselves. Only concerted effort and vigorous management can hope to contain these expenditures within reasonable limits.

It may also be increasingly difficult for colleges and universities in the next 25 years to balance the expenditures of auxiliary enterprises with income from these services. The rising costs of food and of energy have occurred at a time when the number of full-time students living on campus in institutionally owned facilities may begin to decline. Where enrollments have declined, there has been an excess of housing capacity; some alternative uses of facilities and alternative sources of income have become imperative. Balancing income and outgo in intercollegiate athletics will become increasingly difficult as demands for women's participation in athletics grow, and the whole operation of intercollegiate athletics will have to be carefully controlled in order to prevent a deficit operation. Other auxiliary enterprises will have to be managed with equal care.

Universities with medical schools will have to be increasingly concerned with the operating costs of teaching hospitals, whether wholly owned by the university or affiliated with the university. The costs in delivering health care have continued to mount, while third-party payments and patient payments have tended to fall short of hospital and medical expenditures. There is a whole new class of persons in the United States, the medically indigent, who cannot or do not meet the costs of hospital and medical care provided to them. These costs must then be met by government or private contributions. Oftentimes state and local governments have been unable to subsidize in full the gap between the patient payments (direct and third-party) and the operating expenditures of a health science center. More and more attention will have to be given to the financial circumstances of hospital operations.

It is assumed that federal and state agencies, in the very few instances where they are involved, will continue to meet all the operating expenses (direct and support) of independent operations. Universities that manage such facilities and activities on behalf of government agencies will need to be certain that all costs are being met by contract payments. Otherwise, universities will have no choice except to discontinue their management of these independent operations. It is obvious that the financial concerns of higher education institutions will be of major importance during the remainder of this century.

Toward a New Interdependence

Ernest L. Boyer

Prophecy, a wit once remarked, is always dangerous—especially about the future. When I am asked to peer into what American higher education might look like in the year 2000, I feel a bit like Robert Benchley who, during a final exam at Harvard, was required to discuss the "arbitration of the conflict over off-shore fishing rights" from both the British and the U.S. points of view. Writing in his exam book that he knew nothing about either position, he added: "I, therefore, should like to discuss the problem from the viewpoint of the fish."

From the fish-bowl perspective of a university chancellor, I can only venture some murky speculations about the future of higher education as we move toward AD 2000. Since Harvard College was founded in 1636, American education has passed through two major periods, each with a distinct flavor. The first era, beginning with Harvard, lasted over two centuries: There were no high schools. Our early colleges, small and usually church-related and often run by a minister, enrolled teen-age boys (as young as 14) from well-to-do families. These adolescent scholars pursued a cut-and-dried curriculum—all learned Greek and Latin—and then moved on, at 18 or so, as preachers, teachers, lawyers, doctors, or into other upper-class pursuits.

By the middle of the nineteenth century, the second era had begun—marked by expanding enrollment, a more diverse social base, and an enlarged sense of educational mission. In the wake of westward migration, scores of colleges sprang up. Some died, but more survived to serve a burgeoning democracy. The 1850s saw the first state agricultural college (Lansing, Michigan), the first two Negro colleges (Lincoln and Wilberforce), and Elmira College, which gave the first degrees to women. In the Civil War year of 1862, Abraham Lincoln signed the Land Grant College Act that linked the public university to the soil; and in New York, Ezra Cornell was to propose the founding of "an institution where any person can find instruction in any study."

Since World War II college doors have opened to those of every race and class, and the proportion of high school graduates going on to college has shifted from one in six to one in two. Today over eight million young Americans—almost half of those 18 to 21—are enrolled in higher education.

In the 1960s a new community college sprang up in America every 10 days. And in the 20-year period from 1950 to 1970, higher education expenditures rose from $3 billion to $31 billion, increasing (with adjustments for inflation) almost fivefold.

Inequalities, of course, persist. Four men attend college for every three women. And in the country as a whole, the proportion of whites who embark on higher education still remains roughly twice that of blacks. For the Spanish-speaking and for American Indians, the disparities are worse. But the *principle* and the *goal*— if not yet the total practice—of full educational opportunity for all have gained wide acceptance. Turning to the future, as we move toward AD 2000, it seems clear that higher education is about to enter a *third* period, and major shifts are certain to occur.

First, there will be a fundamental change in our idea about the kind of student to be served. And this shift will relate directly to changes in the ways people organize their lives. We have habitually chopped up the span of human life into slices like a great salami. First, there was a thin slice—12 to 20 years long—devoted almost exclusively to school and perhaps college. Next, there was the thickest chunk—for full-time work. And after that: retirement, the little nubbin at the end. These separate stages were kept rigidly apart and we moved inexorably from stage to stage.

In our desire to conform to this life pattern, we built schools and colleges only for the young. Classes were scheduled Monday through Friday, nine to four, coinciding with the world of work. Students were expected to pursue their studies full time before they entered the adult world, never to return. To be a college dropout turned into a stinging social stigma, a label to be avoided at all cost. Now all this has begun to change, and the implications for higher education are enormous. Consider, for example, the changes among the very young. Today about 40 percent of all boys and girls enroll in prekindergarten programs. Thousands now watch "Sesame Street" and "The Electric Company" at home. The rigid lines between the so-called play years and the school years are vanishing.

The life pattern of older children has changed also. They now mature physically two full years earlier than did their grandparents 50 years ago. If Booth Tarkington were writing *Seventeen* today, he would have to title it *Fifteen*. College students can now vote, and they have as of this writing the right of legal contract in 43 of our 50 states. Some students leave college early or enroll only for part-time study, trying to break out of the educational straitjacket that seems to condemn them to endless incubation. It is a startling and significant fact that in 1975 over 55 percent of all those enrolled in postsecondary education were part-time students. Obviously, the so-called college years are becoming less and less well defined.

To add to this confusion, the well-ordered adult world of work is also beginning to break up. In 1900 the average American workweek was 62 hours; by 1945 it had dropped to 43, and today it is 37½ hours. An even shorter four-day workweek is now beginning to emerge. When we regain full employment, we will increasingly face the problem of what to do with our leisure time.

The lifestyle of older people is changing. We hear a lot about how we have moved from a baby boom to a baby bust, but we should also look at the opposite end of the population curve. Life expectancy has increased from 47 years in 1900 to 71 in 1973, and it is estimated that by 2000 nearly 30 percent of our population will be over 50. In addition, many older people, outdistanced by the pace of change, are being eased or forced into premature retirement during still productive years. This wasteful retirement pattern is tragic in human terms.

For years we have simply assumed that life for all of us was neatly programmed: the early days of freedom, then formal education, then work, then the abrupt click of the pasture gate. We quite properly built schools and colleges to fit this rigid cycle, servicing principally the young and unattached. But these rigidities are breaking up, and it seems clear that by the year 2000 higher education will be viewed not as a four-year prework *stage* of life, but as a continuing *process* to be pursued from 16 to 85.

This brings me to a second prediction: *As education redefines the student to be served, the pattern of our institutions will inevitably change as well.* New educational calendars, new techniques of learning, and new locations for study will be commonplace in the year 2000. For example, it seems clear that in the future more students will leave college early to test the water in the world of work. This will be a planned interruption of the college experience—a kind of step-out (to replace the old dropout stigma) to provide the student with added perspective and maturity. What I envision is an arrangement that would allow all kinds of people to begin their working lives earlier—with intervals of service and travel—before they finish their degrees. It would assume that step-outs are not casualties and failures but the harbingers of quite a new view of the connection between education and real life.

Education will also establish new partnerships with industry and labor to intersperse formal and informal study throughout the working years. Both employers and employees are discovering that neither pure leisure nor pure work is fully satisfying. With increased leisure time, many employees often find themselves at loose ends. In his recent book *Working*, Studs Terkel suggests that "unfulfilling work may have touched malignantly the soul of our society." Looking ahead, I suspect that labor contracts of the 1980s and beyond will include agreements for continued learning arrangements that will free the worker for several hours or more a week to take a college course in his or her factory, store, or laboratory—not only specialized technical courses but liberal studies as well.

I foresee a period when sabbaticals for workers, professionals, and executives will be available as they already are in France and West Germany—regular periods for many people to refine their skills, to pursue long-neglected areas of interest, and to explore intellectual and cultural resources. I also foresee new programs for people in the retirement years. Increasingly, retirement will come to be viewed for what it is: a potentially productive and often vigorous period of life, ideal for further exploration of the world of learning. As zero population growth empties more residence halls on our campuses, they can be used to accommodate older persons interested in learning opportunities and activities in the arts.

Older people unable to come to the campus will not be written off. As we can go into the factories to teach, so also will we go into the nursing homes and the retirement villages. Should we allow a person, after a lifetime of productive work and experience, to vegetate intellectually simply because of the physical impairments of age? Who will pay for all of this? The learner, if he can. But if he cannot? We have Medicare for the body; why not Educare for the mind? The cost would be modest. The returns, in the enrichment of a difficult and often barren state of life, could be enormous. A Right-to-Learn commitment in our national life would recognize that learning and human dignity should walk hand in hand.

Another change is likely to occur. I can envision the day when, along with their diplomas, we give college graduates a Certificate for Continued Learning, a kind of educational credit card valid for life, entitling them to further study on many campuses.

As these and other new patterns emerge, the individual will gain—but our universities also will profit. No longer will our campuses be youth ghettos, viewed by others with suspicion. Students, in turn, will look with less skepticism and anxiety toward the world beyond the campus. Indeed, the time will come when town and gown truly mix, and college will be a place where people of all ages move freely in and out. A college community that *is* a more representative community will then emerge.

Still, a nagging and age-old question remains: *Education to what end?* With all of our success in higher education, we are left with a paradox. At the same time that we have opened college doors wide, expanded the curriculum, and broken down the artificial barriers of time and place, the fundamental purposes underlying all this effort become increasingly obscured. Well before we reach the year 2000, we will be asking once again not only, Who should go to college? but, What should students take with them when they leave?

Since the ancient Greeks, men have believed that to be educated was somehow to be made better. The educated person respected the inheritance of the past, appreciated the realm of arts and letters, and communicated with both skill and grace. Flawed and naive as it may have been, this lofty vision led to a so-called core of common study for all students. In the Academy of Plato, rhetoric, philosophy, and mathematics were the prerequisites to statecraft. In the great universities of the Middle Ages, grammar, logic, rhetoric, music, astronomy, and geometry were the vital center. Most American colleges, in earlier days, offered a common core of classics and Christian doctrine with a smattering of mathematics thrown in.

Until the 1920s, the centerpiece on most campuses was the moral philosophy course taught by the college president, who was often a minister: President Maclean at Princeton said that "if he could find an able scholar who was a Presbyterian he would get him; if no such man was available he would secure a Presbyterian who was *not* an able scholar." Today, the notion of a single set of purposes for all students seems quaint and the so-called common core has been replaced almost everywhere by the free elective system, introduced in 1872 by President Eliot at Harvard. Research has become a major component of the university, thanks to the German influence imported late in the nineteenth century by Eliot and Johns Hopkins. Community service has burgeoned in the post-World War II era. And, of course, religion as an academic discipline has all but disappeared.

Efforts to reverse these trends flickered and then died. The Harvard general education program of the 1940s unabashedly concerned itself with the content of education. The premise was that all citizens (at least all Harvard students) should have some common binding understanding of the roots of their culture and their heritage so that they could enrich it further and protect it from barbarians and zealots. But at most great liberal arts colleges today, only traces of this noble venture can be found.

During the middle 1960s, Columbia tried to revive interest in this issue, and Daniel Bell produced a searching analysis of the goals of education. But the faculty showed so little interest that Lionel Trilling called this "a sad and significant event in the culture of our time." Clearly, we have come a long way since President Maclean assembled a closed-shop faculty of Presbyterians at Princeton. The general education ideal, already weakened, was battered by the social and political upheavals of the 1960s. During this tumultuous decade it was the important, urgent, and essential drive for open access which became the new and central goal of higher learning. But in the process, the larger goals and purposes of education were aggressively pushed aside.

Now a new kind of urgency confronts us. The issue quite simply is survival. There is a growing recognition that the future prospects for both man and nature are in peril and that higher education has a special obligation to respond. As Robert Heilbroner asked in the *New York Review of Books*: "There is a question in the air, a question so disturbing that I would hesitate to ask it aloud did I not believe it existed unvoiced in the minds of many: Is there hope for man?"

Heilbroner's question may focus on the issue a bit too sharply; yet one need not be negative to suggest that we may have reached a point in history when it is no longer possible to assume that some cosmic United Fund guarantees our future. Not merely the chronic doomsayers but also a host of clear-eyed analysts suggest that through a myriad of unintended actions, we may be foreclosing the possibility of life on earth—or so narrowing it that a paralysis of the human spirit is as likely as a nuclear Armageddon.

I believe that time has come to formulate a new, unified central purpose for education, a purpose that can help us understand more clearly the interdependency of peoples and institutions in our world—not just in an ecological sense, but in a social sense as well. Our goal should be to stir within students a global urgency, alerting them to the awesome challenges civilization will confront in the decades just ahead. In proposing this new thrust, I do not suggest that a novel set of courses be required of all students. I am not urging that we again restrict the Princeton faculty to Presbyterians, nor am I denigrating in the slightest the work of thousands of dedicated faculty who already are dealing so vitally with the thorny problems of our era. I am not suggesting that we introduce a new elitism that would reduce support for the broad range of programs which now prepare all manner of students for all manner of worthwhile work.

What I am suggesting is that we move toward a new convergence in higher learning—one that goes beyond the smorgasbord of free electives and focuses on such basic issues as our global supply of food and water, the population problem, energy: its origin and distribution (as in mass transportation), and other, subtler circumstances that influence the quality of our lives. The goal would be a new kind of liberal learning—which draws upon the wisdom of the past, organizes appropriately the knowledge of the present, and focuses sharply on alternatives for the future. Such a program would be rooted in the arts and sciences and in research, but new common core academic programs and new linkages among the current fields of study also would be provided. Specialized courses to inform the faculty, all-campus lecturers and midyear seminars for all students, and carefully selected field experiences—all would be helpful as colleges and universities sought to introduce this new dimension on the campus.

We simply must do a better job of alerting our students to the larger contours of their world, of helping them see the broader ramifications of their actions, and of conveying the urgent need to marshal all our resources as we confront the critical choices of the future. Is there hope for man? Of course there is, provided we can extricate ourselves from immediate preoccupations that loom so large, to confront creatively the issues that urgently press upon us.

The irony here is that we already know the scope of the challenge we now face. The world has 27 days' worth of reserve food supply, and the earth's population now multiplies by 95 million each year. We burn up millions of irreplaceable and unaffordable barrels of oil a day, and the nuclear threat remains. These realities suggest that we must reaffirm the very old notion that the whole human being is more important than each of its parts.

A friend suggested to a former college dean that scientists might soon be able to sever the human brain from the rest of the body and, with appropriate machinery, keep it alive indefinitely with no connection to the heart. "That's nothing new," replied the dean. "We've been doing it on our campus for many years!" The dean's witty comment touches on a vital issue. In recent decades we have concentrated enormous energies on enlarging the physical capacity of our colleges, so that the democratic ideal might be more fully realized for more people. That commitment must remain central to our purpose. But we must now also turn to another task: that of defining with more clarity—and perhaps more passion—the large social meaning, the broader human purpose, of this massive effort.

So as I look toward the year 2000, I see an education program that will serve new people—men and women from all walks of life—through recurrent education from ages 16 to 85. I see an education program with new patterns: with step-outs, sabbaticals, and with courses in the home, the factory, and on the TV screen. I see a program of education with new purposes: with a special focus on the ways we may survive with dignity on the planet earth.

Beyond all this I have a deep and abiding faith that as men and women—rich and poor, young and old—begin to learn together and deliberate the new central issues of our time and of our future, a network of educational town meetings will emerge across the land. As we begin to talk and plan together, a new sense of interdependence will stir among us and, as it does, prospects for humanity in the year 2000 may become brighter than they seem today.

Autonomy on the Line

Ralph K. Huitt

Higher education in America faces the last quarter of the twentieth century in the firm embrace of our big, friendly federal government. That, in my opinion, is its most serious problem. The giver is the governor. The ultimate sanction—the withholding of funds—is lethal. Accommodations will be made to avoid it. The minions of the government, meanwhile, many of them innocent of experience and knowledge of the institutional life of higher education, roam the campus issuing their decrees. Multiple agencies enforce the same legislative acts and the cost of their governance increases. We seem to be in the process of creating an anomaly of political theory—an authoritarian, totalitarian, representative government. It is authoritarian already, totalitarian not yet, and representative indeed. For it must not be forgotten that behind every act of the government there are effective groups that want it to do what it does. The power of the government over the private lives of people grows because so many of us want to use its authority to accomplish what we believe to be good.

The states, of course, should not be disregarded. They still provide a large part of the funding of postsecondary education, and their officials want a say in how it is run. They want the use of precious resources to be planned wisely, carried out efficiently, and accounted for honestly. These processes will increasingly include private education as private institutions come to share more and more in the resources of the states. It is quite true that if a person is educated in a private institution the public purpose is served as effectively as if he had been educated in a public school. It is also true that if the private institution answers to the state on admissions, curriculum, teacher-student ratios, and many other matters, the difference between private and public grows very thin. And that would be a heavy loss. The autonomy and integrity of the independents is needed by us all. Most of us say that the special contribution of the private schools must be preserved, even as they become less independent; but no one, so far as I know, has said how that is to be done.

Happily, there are other developments that may benefit all who share in the life of higher education. One is the willingness to learn new ways of educating people and with it the recruitment of new kinds of people to the joys and enhancement of life afforded by higher education. For a long time it seemed that colleges and universities would forever believe that the only valid learning experience came from a professor lecturing to seated students who reproduced his notes imperfectly and tried to recall them at specified times. That notion has been pretty well exploded by now, though without joy in many quarters. The contention that through creative innovation we could devise other ways to teach opened up opportunities for many who had found the traditional classroom beyond their reach: part-time students, for example, who in sheer numbers are already gaining on full-time, some of whom want credits and degrees, some not; professionals wishing to refresh their skills; persons seeking occupational advancement; and many others who simply want to enhance the quality of their lives.

Altogether, one of the magnificent achievements of this century has been the extension of opportunity—not the least of which is in higher education—to millions of people who had hitherto not had it. When one thinks of this movement toward the realization of the promise of American life, it is hard to say that government interference is too high a price to pay.

It should be added hastily that the growth of nontraditional education does not render the campus obsolete. Quite the contrary. Students learn from other students and, sometimes for the first time in their lives, begin to share in the intellectual and cultural treasures of their society. Indeed, a college or university campus is a nourishing mother to the large community that has access to it. The value of nontraditional education is not simply that it extends that community (which it does), but also that it gives campus-bound teaching a chance to explore new and better ways.

Finally, what about money? A television interviewer who asked me recently what was the number one problem in higher education was astonished that I did not say finances. We have cried so much that it is a little embarrassing so many institutions are still open. There is a problem, of course, and it bears unevenly on various institutions. But this society has supported and will continue to support higher education. Its commitment to college and university education is as astonishing as it is heartening. The long period of protest and violence on the campuses did not bring punitive legislation nor appropriations. A congressional education appropriation in 1976 proved to be one of the rare legislative acts which was passed over a Presidential veto. Many states significantly increased their funding of their public institutions in 1975. If the year 2000 finds colleges and universities in a parlous state, it will not be because the American people refused to fund them.

The end of the century can be faced, it seems to me, without undue optimism or foreboding. The homogenizing hand of government may well prove to be more than society generally is willing to bear and higher education may share in a common relief. The innovative and traditional elements on the campuses may join in an honest marriage which will enable both to achieve their potential to enrich life and expand human productivity. What seems more likely, if one considers the dynamism of the system, is that the future will be something not dreamed of now.

The View From the Hill

Carl D. Perkins

Education today is a product of the educational trends of the 1950s and 1960s—trends so closely interwoven with world-wide developments in government, media, civil rights, science, and technology that any accurate prediction must also take these areas into consideration. To do so obviously calls for clairvoyance. In the absence of this gift, one must then use whatever special information one has, and interpret it from the perspective of one's particular vantage point.

My own vantage point is that of a legislator deeply involved in the development of federal education policy and legislation for over 25 years. Some may consider this the periphery of American education, while others may view the federal contribution as quite substantial. That there is a disparity in view is understandable, for the federal role has been somewhat inconsistent.

At times it would appear that the government has been a relatively passive partner, responding occasionally, and at a snail's pace, to developments that have already occurred. For example, the need for federal financial assistance for the construction of academic facilities for our nation's colleges and universities was well documented as early as 1958. But it was not until 1963—when President Kennedy pointed out that "the long predicted crisis in higher education facilities is now at hand"—that any relief from the federal level was finally authorized.

By contrast, there have been times when the federal government has assumed an active role, urging and motivating change in education policy and practice. Few will deny the stimulus provided compensatory education for disadvantaged students as a result of Title I of the Elementary and Secondary Education Act of 1965. Not only were compensatory programs and services extended, expanded, and in many instances established for the first time with millions of federal dollars, but, equally important, local attitudes and policies were changed by this new federal interest and focus.

While there is a difference in view as to the impact of the federal role in education, few will quarrel with the assertion that federal involvement has been steadily increasing. The federal commitment to postsecondary education had its origins back in the nineteenth century with the use of land grants to support state universities. The funneling of federal support to specific programs for higher education institutions did not begin until the early 1900s, however. In fact, both institutional and student eligibility for federal higher education programs at first was narrow in scope.

The enactment of the Servicemen's Readjustment Act of 1944— better known as the GI Bill—opened higher education to veterans after World War II and radically expanded the profile of the college student. While the GI Bill was narrow in the sense that aid was targeted to one group, it had pervasive implications for future student aid programs for it opened postsecondary opportunities to a whole new range of students.

The backbone of the expansionary process for student aid was unquestionably the National Defense Education Act (NDEA) student loan program—landmark legislation not because of its scope or size, but because of the unprecedented policies and directions it represented. With the NDEA began what was to become a very strong legislative push to increase accessibility to postsecondary education for all citizens. Although selection of student borrowers under the loan program was at first based on superior academic backgrounds in science, mathematics, engineering, or modern foreign languages, the program later became more flexible and has grown more than thirtyfold from nearly 25,000 students to over 834,000 students receiving benefits annually.

Passage of the Higher Education Act of 1965 marked the beginning of a victory in a difficult uphill struggle for education opportunity for all Americans. It not only expanded student aid for the disadvantaged through educational opportunity grants and the college work-study program but it also provided support to institutions through college library programs, subsidies for instructional equipment, strengthening of developing institutions, and expansionary amendments to the program of grants and loans to assist in the construction of academic facilities.

The Education Amendments of 1972, at least for federal purposes and assistance, expanded considerably on the traditional concepts of higher education institutions and students. The term "postsecondary education" was utilized throughout the act rather than the more traditional term "higher education." The change was not only in name but also in substance, for it indicated that the federal interest extended far beyond the "typical" 18- to 21-year-old college student enrolled in a traditional four-year program of undergraduate work.

In the 1972 amendments perhaps the most revolutionary idea was the establishment of a program of grants to students based more on the financial circumstances of the student than on the costs at the institution he or she wished to attend. In the few years since its inception, the program has grown to a point where today some 1.6 million students are receiving aid.

Perhaps the growth of the federal involvement in education can best be illustrated by citing the history of appropriations for the U.S. Office of Education. One hundred years ago, appropriations for education totaled $45,570. Fifty years later, funding grew to approximately $11.6 million—about 255 times the original amount! It took 25 years to bring the total to $138 million in 1951. The enactment of the Impacted Aid program that year had led to an increase of over $100 million in a single year. From 1950 to 1975, such growth occurred that today the appropriations bill for the Education Division of the Department of Health, Education, and Welfare totals $7.5 billion. In this 25-year period, appropriations have increased more than 54 times.

The increase in federal involvement is not only in terms of dollars, however. Recent enactments such as the Family Rights and Privacy Act, and Title IX of the Education Amendments prohibiting discrimination on the basis of sex, are specific enactments dealing with educational problems of a totally different nature. Moreover, because education is one of the largest businesses in America, more general enactments—such as occupational health and safety, environmental protection, minimum wage, equal employment, affirmative action, Social Security, and pensions—are also having considerable impact on American postsecondary education.

If there is any certainty as to the course of postsecondary education over the next 25 years it is that costs will continue to increase. Financial problems have already compelled some colleges to close their doors or to merge, and it is inevitable as costs continue to rise that more institutions will fall by the wayside.

The financial crisis in postsecondary education is not only restricted to institutions, for family after family has found itself with its own financial crisis in struggling to cope with spiraling postsecondary educational costs. These increasing costs have already had an impact on choice. In the last decade, total enrollments grew by 88 percent; in the community and junior college sector the increase has exceeded 230 percent.

Within institutions we are experiencing changes in the composition of the student population. A combination of student-aid policies and increased costs creates a situation where education in the private sector is more and more the prerogative only of the very financially needy students and the well-to-do.

It is more difficult to anticipate the future with respect to enrollments. The Carnegie Council has projected that the total enrollment by the year 2000 will reach 13.2 million, compared to 8.6 million in 1970. Of those 13 million the Carnegie Council projected that 11.2 million would be in prebaccalaureate study and nearly 2 million in postbaccalaureate study. However, the new growth is predicted to be sporadic rather than a continuation of the very steady growth pattern that doubled the postsecondary education population every 14 to 15 years for the past century.

Another consideration is the identity of postsecondary students of the future. There has already been a tremendous change. Until very recently, everyone thought of the college student as being 18 to 21 years of age. This is no longer the case. Education is becoming a lifelong process. Increased lifespans contribute to this process, making it possible for more and more older Americans to seek educational opportunities for professional as well as personal reasons. Statistics bear this out. According to the Bureau of the Census, "The most dramatic increase in college enrollment in the 1970s has been among older students.... Although half of the college students were still 18 to 21 years old, students 25 years old and over comprised one third of all students in 1974... [and] one million were 35 years old and over. The older student (25 and over) made up about two thirds of all part-time students and one sixth of the full-time students."

Clearly, postsecondary education has become more accessible to a greater variety of Americans. The full-time 18- to 21-year-old student, once the standard figure in the student population, is becoming the minority in the total postsecondary education population. In 1970, 29 percent of the total college population studied part time. In 1976, that percentage grew to 38.6 percent.

If, during the next 25 years, postsecondary education continues to experience increasing costs, accessibility, and enrollments—and I believe that it will—we will at the same time see a continuing increase in the role of the federal government.

With respect to accessibility, government has been an active partner. The commitment to full access is now a well-entrenched tradition and the federal government will continue to be both interested and active in the encouragement of this goal. As costs continue to rise for both institutions and students, the demand for greater federal assistance will increase proportionately. Likewise, increasing enrollments and continuing changes in student populations suggest an increasing federal role.

As that role increases during the next 25 years, the need for flexibility in federal policy is obvious. The validity of the hard-and-fast roles that have been foundations of educational policy for decades can be seen melting away at an alarmingly fast rate. The simple fact is that unless we continue to allow for changes in student goals, in student populations, and in educational costs, federal legislation may very well find itself obsolete even before it is enacted.

Second, as we look to the future, the federal government must resist the temptation to continue adding agency after agency and program after program where already existing machinery can be more effectively utilized. We must resist proposals that call for elaborate new mechanisms to handle every new problem.

Undoubtedly there will be new needs that the federal government will have to meet with new legislative programs, but we must evaluate first whether the best solution may be the refinement of existing mechanisms. We must be careful not to negate the effectiveness of the overall federal involvement by making it highly cumbersome or unworkable.

Third, we must create policy that in addition to being flexible and uncomplicated is sensitive to the uniqueness of American postsecondary education. Diversity, autonomy, and excellence are concepts deeply embedded in our postsecondary education system, and the federal government must respect and appreciate them.

These suggested guidelines for federal policy do not respond to the more important question of how much financial responsibility the federal government should or will shoulder in the years ahead. Today the federal financial responsibility in postsecondary education approximates 15 percent. Assuming that the policy guidelines suggested above will be followed, I would hope that the percentage could be increased to at least one third.

The battle to establish an appropriate level of spending for postsecondary education has been going on for a long time. Notwithstanding the landmark legislation enacted in the last 25 years, that battle is still far from over. It is in essence—when all of the emotion and oratory are stripped away—a matter of priorities; a matter of establishing how important education is when measured against all the other highly competitive needs of a society heading into the twenty-first century.

The basic response to challenges that will face postsecondary education will have to come from its own internal genius. In large part the extent of the federal commitment will depend on the extent to which educators and legislators work in a united effort in seeing to it that education gets its fair share of this nation's resources.

By making sure that the federal role is flexible, simple, sensitive, and commensurate with the need, we can be reasonably certain that 25 years from now—regardless of the changes brought about in society by forces beyond the control of educators and their institutions—we will have a system of postsecondary education that meets the needs of all individuals.

The goal is to reach a point at which every citizen in the United States who wants a postsecondary education will have the opportunity to pursue the type of education he or she desires, regardless of personal, financial, or other inhibiting circumstances. Only in this way will each individual be able to make an optimum contribution to American society.

III
Equality and Excellence

Higher Education
and Human Equality

Howard R. Bowen

One of the driving forces of present-day American society is the belief that wide differences among people in income, power, privilege, and status are unjust. While the Declaration of Independence and Tocqueville teach us that the quest for human equality is not a new feature in American life, at no time in the past has the demand for equality been so pervasive or persistent as it is today. Virtually every group that has endured inferiority of social position is now pressing for equality—workers, farmers, racial and ethnic groups, women, the poor, the handicapped, teen-agers, the elderly, homosexuals, drug users, convicts, and many others. Their demands have not gone wholly unheeded, and there is a vast array of social legislation designed to assure civil rights, outlaw certain forms of discrimination, tax the rich, subsidize the poor, and, not least, extend education.

Education at all levels has long been regarded as a key element in the quest for equality. It has been thought to operate in at least three ways. First, education has been viewed as a portal through which the children of all classes would find equal opportunity in the contest for social position. Second, it has been generally believed that the widening of education to include more people, and the deepening of education to increase their learning, would narrow the differences in competency and in socialization, and would lessen inequality of social position. Third, education has been viewed as a source of political strength in the drive for equality. Many believed it would help underprivileged people become conscious of their position, and of the inconsistencies between the ideals and realities of American society; that it would help them to understand how inequality might be ameliorated, and thus to become effective in the political arena. Moreover, they have thought that liberal education for the upper classes would inculcate humane values that would incline them favorably toward egalitarian ideals and policies.

Recently, however, the belief that the diffusion of education might lessen inequality has faced increasing skepticism. It is often noted, for example, that despite the advancement of education, distribution of income has remained remarkably stable over time; and differences in power, privilege, and social status seem not to have noticeably narrowed. Much has been made of the fact that education, through its system of admissions, grades, degrees, and other credentials, performs the function of sorting the population and consigning its members to various occupations and stations in society. It is also argued that persons of the greatest ability and highest socioeconomic status are the very ones who receive the most education and profit most from it. As a result, differences in income and status are if anything magnified by education rather than reduced. Finally it is suggested that education may not be a significant factor in determining the future social position of students. Correlations between amount of education and "success" in later life, when other factors are controlled, are not very high.

These allegations are not wholly consistent with one another, but they do present a formidable basis for questioning the efficacy of education in bringing about equality. They place the burden of proof on those who hold that education does promote human equality.

Most discussions of inequality as related to education refer to inequality of opportunity rather than inequality of condition. These are quite different concepts. There is no assurance that progress toward equality of opportunity would in any way lessen inequality of condition. Equality of opportunity is a worthwhile goal. It would enhance fairness in the contest for social position and it would improve efficiency by placing talent where it is most productive. But it would not significantly lessen inequality of condition. It would only rearrange the population. If every vestige of discrimination based on race, ethnicity, sex, age, physical appearance, and so on were eliminated, inequality of condition would not be significantly lessened. Many women, members of minority groups, and other underprivileged persons would rise in the rank order, but many white men would be placed lower and the form of the overall distribution of people according to social position would be unchanged. I shall thus consider higher education with regard to equality of condition, not equality of opportunity.

Some skepticism is in order about the possibility—or even the desirability—of promoting equality of condition. First, history teaches us that progress toward equality of condition is not easy. Most industrial societies have been characterized by wide divergence among their people with respect to social position. Inequality of condition has a way of surviving even the most well-intentioned and thoroughgoing welfare and educational programs, religious and moral crusades, and even violent social revolutions. The inertial forces seem overwhelming, and temporary gains have a way of vanishing in the long run. The idealism behind programs for equality is usually no match for avarice, pride, and lust for power. Second, progress toward equality of condition—especially if it levels down from the top—may be achieved at the expense of cultural and intellectual excellence; or at the cost of incentives needed for productivity; or at the risk of government controls that jeopardize freedom. Third, objective changes in the degree of inequality may not be perceived by the population. People are highly sensitive to differences among themselves, and statistically small differences can still be the basis for enormous invidious distinctions.

Social equality may be elusive. Yet the same human beings who are afflicted with the sins of avarice, pride, and lust for power— namely, all of us to some extent—also have a saintly side that values brotherhood, charity, and justice. Egalitarianism in contemporary society is an expression of this side of human nature. It calls on the rich, the proud, and the powerful to share with the poor, the lowly, and the weak, and it entitles the latter to press for brotherhood and justice. And it calls upon everyone to seek equality in the faith that greater justice, both in fact and in perception, is possible and that justice can be reconciled with cultural excellence, incentives for productivity, and freedom. The call is especially compelling for educators.

There are three ways to narrow inequality among persons. One is to change people in ways that will tend to make them less unequal in their basic abilities and traits and that in turn will lessen inequality with respect to social position. A second way is to change the perceptions of people as to what constitutes inequality. A third way is to redress the inequality in society by redistributing income and other benefits that are in the first instance unequally apportioned. I shall consider only the first of these methods, changing people, which is of course the business of education. Surely it is also the most desirable way of reducing inequality. By changing people so that differences among them in basic abilities and traits are lessened, then differences are narrowed in what people are, in what they can contribute to society, and in what they get by way of income and social position.

Genetic changes. The range of differences among people might be reduced through control of genetic factors. Persons with known genetic defects of a crippling sort might be required or persuaded not to procreate. Possibilities may be opening up for genetic engineering through which defective genes could be repaired. There is little enthusiasm in America for pressing these methods very far, but some reduction in inequality by reducing the number of people with serious genetic defects seems possible.

Changes in socioeconomic background. The range of differences among persons might be reduced also by overcoming the crippling effects of adverse socioeconomic conditions, especially adverse family and neighborhood environments. The socioeconomic backgrounds of disadvantaged people might be raised through improvements in nutrition, housing, neighborhood environment, health care, and education. For those already handicapped by adverse socioeconomic background, compensatory measures can be taken in the form of early childhood education, special programs for teen-agers, adult education and job training, and preferential admission to higher education.

Efforts along these lines have been made for generations, and have been intensified in the past two decades. The results are far from reassuring. Partly because change among the disadvantaged is slow, and partly because gains made at the lower end of the social scale in education, health, and so on tend to be matched by gains at the upper end of the scale, the overall degree of inequality has remained the same.

To conclude that such efforts are ineffective, however, is undoubtedly premature. Knowledge of how to proceed is inadequate and the resources applied have been limited. But even with well-conceived programs and sufficient resources, progress is bound to be slow. The idea that millions of people can be changed instantly through crash programs with limited resources is an illusion. Progress must be measured in decades, not in years.

Change through education. As I have indicated, the efforts to raise people at the lower end of the scale through education seem not to lessen inequality because people at the upper end of the scale are also advancing and differences remain unchanged. For this reason, inequality of educational attainment has not been lessened in the last few decades. But the recent past has been a transitional period and is not necessarily a precursor of the distant future.

Historic changes in educational attainment may be viewed in three stages. The first was typified by the American frontier where differences in education were small because almost no one had much. The range, with few exceptions, was from illiteracy to fourth grade. There were differences, of course, in other aspects of socioeconomic background and in what was learned through experience. But differences in formal education on the whole were quite small.

The second stage, through which we are now passing, has been a period in which differences in educational level have become very great. The adult population now ranges from illiterates and recent immigrants with limited educational backgrounds to persons with PhDs, and there are many people at every intermediate level. During this second stage the whole population has not been advancing together in educational level, one grade at a time. While the educational level of young people has been increasing rapidly, that of older people has not changed much, and the educational progress of some groups of young people has been much more rapid than that of others, the difference being largely related to differences in socioeconomic background. The result is a very unequal distribution of educational attainment.

In the third stage, which we are now slowly approaching, virtually the entire population will have completed several years of high school; one half to two thirds will have attended college; and perhaps 10 percent will have obtained some postbaccalaureate study. At this third stage, the differences in educational level can be expected to diminish because nearly everyone will have achieved considerable education.

These changes in the distribution of educational attainment may be illustrated in the following table showing estimated percentages of the adult population by education levels at various historic stages:

	Grade School: 0 to 8th grade	High School: 9th to 12th grade	College: 13th grade or above	Total
Stage I, 1825 (hypothetical)	95%	4%	1%	100%
Stage II, 1975 (actual)	23%	53%	24%	100%
Stage III, 2025 (projected)	3%	37%	60%	100%

As shown in the table, educational attainment was distributed quite equally at Stage I in that most of the population had very little of it. It will again be distributed quite equally at Stage III when virtually all the population will have a great deal of it. But at present, in transitional Stage II, differences in educational level are very great (perhaps just past the maximum). The process of moving large numbers from lower levels of education to higher levels of education can only be accomplished over several generations. One of the costs of going through Stage II is a widening of educational differences and a concomitant widening of differences in social position. Little wonder that inequality is today a major social issue.

It may be imagined that the transitional process will go on indefinitely as more people seek advanced education. But this trend is limited by the fact that formal education, like other kinds of resource use, is subject to diminishing returns. As one's educational level rises, the incremental gains in desirable abilities and traits diminish. This is reflected in the fact that additions to income, power, privilege, and status diminish as education is lengthened. Studies of the economic return on education uniformly show that the return is greatest at the elementary level, next at the secondary level, next at the college level, and least at the higher levels. The reason for this is that people can scarcely function in an industrial society without the elementary rudiments of literacy and "numeracy." But at each subsequent stage of education the economic returns fall because cost rises and the incremental benefits decline.

Diminishing returns also occur as a result of the extension of higher education to more people. As more people receive college education, the supply of persons available for the preferred positions in our society increases and the salaries and prestige from these positions tend to fall; correspondingly, the number of less-educated persons available for the less desirable positions declines and their wages rise. For example, the earnings of coal miners and truck drivers may exceed those of teachers and junior bank officers. As a result, the relative economic gain from college diminishes. There is considerable evidence that the relative returns on investments in higher education have been declining in recent years.

As differences in educational levels within the population become narrower, the role of higher education as a credentialing and screening device for job placement will become less important. For example, if almost everyone were a high school graduate, and large numbers had college degrees, then these particular credentials would lose much of their significance for screening and specific qualifications related less closely to formal education would become more important. Also, if higher education were widened and deepened, it would yield less not only in income but also in power, privilege, and status.

The conclusion is that if higher education were extended to more people, inequality would be lessened. On the other hand, if the spread of higher education were to cease, as is often advocated on grounds that there are not enough jobs of the kind traditionally reserved for the college educated, then present differences in educational level and the present degree of inequality would be maintained, and the American dream of equality through education would have been effectively frustrated. To maintain the higher educational system at Stage II would simply perpetuate present inequality.

A common criticism of mass higher education is that only part of the population is qualified for higher learning. This, of course, is true. However, differences in scholastic aptitude are probably due in considerable part to socioeconomic background, which could be changed over time. Indeed, the percentage of the population with scholastic aptitude up to college standards has grown steadily throughout the twentieth century. I have heard informed guesses that if further progress could be made in improving the socioeconomic background of disadvantaged persons, perhaps 75 percent or more of the population would be qualified to do college work at reasonable standards.

The percentage of the population that may be considered educable at the college level will also depend on our conception of higher learning. That conception has been steadily broadening as we have moved from a classical education characteristic of the nineteenth century to an education that encompasses natural sciences, social studies, many interdisciplinary fields, and many professional and vocational areas. The conception has been broadening also as methods of instruction have been diversified to include various forms of independent study, self-paced learning, internships, experiential learning, and mechanized instruction, and as higher education has become increasingly available to older adults and to part-time students of all ages. There are possibilities of broadening the conception even further.

As I have pointed out, however, the present system of higher education is at transitional Stage II. One of its main tasks is to introduce millions of persons of widely varying backgrounds and cultural levels into higher education. As Stage III is approached, and the general educational level of the population becomes higher and more equal, then the student population will again be more homogeneous, and the goals and standards of higher education can be less varied.

At the same time, the degree to which human equality can be approached will be determined in part by the range and variety of interests that are considered in measuring or judging differences among individuals. For example, if differences are measured in terms of a single criterion, such as income, differences will be very pronounced. But if other interests, such as scholarly learning, moral virtue, religious commitment, sociability, artistic talent, skill in handicrafts, a green thumb, civic participation, athletic ability, mechanical skill, and adventurous spirit, were all valued qualities in addition to income, then overall inequality would be greatly lessened. The greater the number of dimensions along which excellence is measured, the less the inequality.

If education were viewed as a way of serving people of widely different traits and abilities, of helping them to discover their talents and interests and values, and of helping them develop themselves along lines compatible with their varied interests, then education could be an instrument for widening the range of human expression and reducing inequality among persons. A pluralistic culture cannot encompass every interest and every temperament; society would simply lose its coherence and integrity. But the range of permitted interests need not be so narrow as to condemn large numbers of its people to the role of incompetents or second-class citizens or deviants. Higher education could be an instrument for broadening our notion of valued interests and thus of reducing the sense of social inequality.

The Question of Access— And to What

Claiborne Pell

The course of change in education has recently run at such a pace and in such an erratic manner that trends are difficult to determine. This stems in part from the very deep involvement of education with the social upheavals affecting our nation, a condition I see quite clearly from a position not as an educator but as a politician.

The involvement of education with social problems is linked to the decline of one of the oldest traditions: education as ivory tower. For the first 200 years of our nation's development, higher education was narrowly defined. Its hallmarks were a heavy emphasis on the classics, a strong religious content, some emphasis on letters, and, generally, an upper-class constituency. It was thought that any man with a foundation in the roots of the Western, Judeo-Christian tradition could succeed at any task life thrust upon him. The influence of the work ethic cannot be overstated: Anyone who worked hard and played by the rules went ahead.

But in recent years, beginning with the New Deal and accelerating after World War II, these precepts have been called into question. The once monolithic educational community has been resolved into hundreds of competing groups, as the composition of the student body became increasingly disparate.

A primary instrument of this development has been the federal government. Millions of veterans attended postsecondary institutions through the GI Bill. Had such federal assistance not been available, a large percentage of these men and women would never have seen the inside of a college classroom. As a result, a much broader spectrum of society began to envision higher education as a right, and they went on to claim that right for their children.

Ten years later, the challenge of Sputnik spurred Congress to question the directions higher education had been taking. Increased emphasis was placed on science and foreign language training, both through funds for institutional programs and through student loan and fellowship assistance. For the first time, low-cost (to the student), broadly based student financial aid was made available by the federal government. It was on this program, the National Defense Student Loan Program, that the next decade of federal aid programs was built.

The expansive years of the New Frontier and the Great Society saw a proliferation of federal programs designed to assist students in postsecondary education. Two major federal policy decisions concerning the form and substance of such aid had a ripple effect on the nature of postsecondary education. First, aid was directed primarily toward students from low-income families, further eroding the upper-class orientation of some institutions. To receive federal money, institutions had to seek out and enroll the poor.

Second, eligibility for student assistance was broadened beyond traditional institutions of higher education to include the wider range of postsecondary educational opportunities, both academic and occupational. Congress decided that students should be able to participate in federal programs regardless of the place or nature of their educations. I would assume that all future federal efforts will take this broad approach toward postsecondary education.

In 1972, Congress faced a major decision on delivery systems for further postsecondary assistance: Should funds be channeled directly to institutions for use in their general operational budgets; or should funds be made available to students through some form of grant assistance, and paid to institutions in tuition and fees? The arguments on both sides were explored at some depth and with not a little intensity of feeling. The decision, perhaps reflecting the increased consumer orientation of our society, came down strongly in favor of providing the money directly to the student. This pattern of federal assistance will continue to grow in the quarter century ahead.

What I have been describing can be summed up by a single word: access. No individual desiring a postsecondary education and capable of benefiting from one should be denied such an education due to economic need. Unfortunately, federal funds have not followed this federal commitment in amounts sufficient to ensure equality of educational opportunity. However, I am hopeful that additional funds will be available in the near future, not only from the federal government, but also from states and the institutions themselves, to make this goal a reality.

The goal of access inevitably leads to the question, Access to what? Pressures from new classes and generations of students, as well as economic pressures, have prompted institutions to make their curricula more "meaningful." As a result, courses are becoming increasingly occupationally oriented. Disciplines with no discernible relevance to careers are being deemphasized. If this trend continues, we will be turning our colleges and universities into trade schools, turning out a work force with a degree but not, to my mind, educated.

That is not to say that career-oriented education should not play a strong role in postsecondary education. Its aims are legitimate: to make graduates employable in the world they will have to face. However, I fear a system that overly emphasizes the relevant and timely while disowning the intellect. There should be a place for great literature as well as for occupational training in the education of each individual. Otherwise, we may be faced with a situation similar to that in Orwell's *1984*, where many people were educated but few were intelligent.

It should be remembered, too, that as education has been thrust into the forefront of today's society, it has contracted many of society's ills. Education is expected simultaneously to cure society's problems—for it is a truism that a better-educated society will be a better society—and to mirror the immediate demands of the people it is intended to serve. Consequently, economic problems, energy crises, the decline of our large cities, and resultant social pressures and animosities all must be addressed if education as we know it is to survive. Schools cannot be asked to do everything; part of their current difficulties is that they have been asked to do too much.

My own commitment to high-quality, universal postsecondary education is strong. Our people and institutions have faced serious challenges in the past; they can meet and overcome the challenges we now face. Basically, we must bear in mind that, in the next 25 years, there will be a larger proportion of college-educated citizens, and that, with increasing technology, each citizen will have more leisure at his disposal. Education, then, should pursue two objectives: the obvious one of preparing students for the competition of the job market and giving them the ability to change jobs in the increasingly mobile employment markets of the future; but also—and equally important—adding substantially to their ability to enjoy life and leisure.

The Interplay
of Mass and Class

Harold Howe II

In the last quarter of the twentieth century our diverse system of
colleges and universities in the United States has more than
enough problems to challenge the energies of its leaders. All the
old questions about what and how best to teach and learn and
who should do so must be answered again for a new generation
facing a world that, from the vantage point of 1976, seems vastly
different than it did 10 or even 5 years ago. I expect and hope that
the answers to these questions will be as diverse as the system itself
and that there will be no single, national response by our institutions of higher education to the problems of the future.

Some institutions will continue to see postsecondary education
as solidly based in the study of mankind's record here on earth,
and will thus seek solid ground for their students in contemplation
of the achievements of both imagination and science; some institutions, concerned with the economic roles of their graduates, will
revamp their programs so as to prepare students to do the kinds of
things they expect society will want done and be willing to pay
for; still other institutions, stating their purposes in terms of broad
problems that are now evident (the environment, reduced economic growth, disparities of wealth and power), will lead their
students to learning within a framework of knowledge and understanding they believe appropriate to these conditions; and some
institutions, seeing more purpose in process than in substance, will
allow their students to design their own education and evaluate
their own progress in it. All these variations and more will in the
next several decades prosper and find adherents.

Perhaps only one generalization can be made with confidence about the curricular aspects of postsecondary education over the next 25 years: They will be in a constant state of ferment because the world around them is in ferment. But the very fact that this is now evident and even shows some likelihood of increasing in the years ahead is itself a healthy sign. A judgment I would make by comparison (and with which some will not agree) is that primary and secondary schooling in the United States has a more massive characteristic and will probably have a more difficult time adjusting itself to those alterations in values, lifestyles, and aspirations that are being pressed upon Americans by forces as diverse as the women's movement, Arab control of oil, environmental hazards, nuclear proliferation, the aspirations of new nations, and the communications revolution.

One reason that postsecondary education is more flexible and adaptable than elementary and secondary eduction is its diversity. It is part private and part public; the public portion of it operates under varying systems within states; and it is characterized by institutions with totally different notions of what constitutes "an education," and with considerable freedom to pursue their programs as they wish. Within recent years it has spawned new types of institutions to serve special clienteles—the community college, for example, or the upper-division college; and it is rapidly demonstrating a new flexibility in reaching previously unserved groups in our society. The lower schools, on the other hand, partake of a common general structure: They are mostly public; their graded characteristic persists despite vigorous criticism; and what they do and the way they do it has a sameness reinforced by textbooks, teacher qualifications, and other common denominators reaching from school to school and state to state.

So I am more hopeful about the capacity of postsecondary education to change in order to meet whatever the twenty-first century has in store. But this is only a relative judgment. Postsecondary education still has plenty of problems. And if I have to select one of them, it lies in the following question: Can our colleges and universities continue the trend of the years 1950-1975, when they pursued more effectively than ever before the principle of equality of opportunity, while at the same time maintaining excellence in teaching, learning, and research?

The interplay of mass and class has long been the subject of argument and speculation and has long had a special place in our history. There are those today who view the development of advanced education for a growing proportion of people as a threat to the finest in our academic tradition; others see it as a broad new avenue for the passage of untapped talent representing groups traditionally denied, by economic, racial, or other barriers, a chance to realize their potential.

The only realistic response to the choice of equality or excellence is to seek both; and there is reason to believe, in spite of the skeptics, that we can do so. Our history says that we can, our traditions and beliefs say that we should, and our national needs say that we must. But we must recognize the inevitable tensions in maintaining both elitist and egalitarian principles at the same time and muster the wisdom and restraint to prevent one from destroying or unduly eroding the other.

The period from 1960 to 1975 can be divided at about 1970 for the purpose of gaining some perspective on the recent interplay of equality and excellence. Before 1970, advanced education experienced genuine growth with regard to both: New constituencies, previously unserved, entered in vast numbers; new institutions to serve them proliferated, particularly the community colleges; and new infusions of private and public money added backing to the quality and scope of research and advanced training at universities long recognized as the country's strongest. In a sense, everything seemed to grow bigger and better, even though a fall was just around the corner.

We turned the corner in 1970 and the fall is still with us. It seems to be characterized by three mutually reinforcing phenomena: a general slowing of growth in higher education, creating what has come to be called "steady state," a condition in which change can no longer be achieved by growth but requires that activities be dropped in order to try new ones; a weakening of confidence in higher education as a source of wisdom for the nation and of economic and personal reward for the individual; a tendency for the egalitarian emphasis of the sixties to grow stronger, while the emphasis on quality diminishes in relative importance. The tendency of excellence in higher education to erode first in times of hardship and self-doubt threatens the healthy balance we must maintain if we aspire, in John Gardner's phrase, to be both equal and excellent at the same time. While the first two of these three points need both comment and interpretation, the third is of the essence for our purposes here. It is a point that requires elaboration in both undergraduate and graduate education, in private as well as public institutions, but in this brief statement, I shall focus only upon those institutions at the heart of it: the major research universities.

For the past several years, the signals from the research universities of the United States, both public and private, have been clear enough to anyone who would listen. These institutions have been through internal processes of self-discipline that initially removed inefficiencies and then began to truncate their missions and limit the quality of teaching, learning, and research. Schools and departments have been dropped, to advantage in some instances; in others, hard compromises with fiscal reality (created by annual cost increases of 8 percent while annual income grew at only 5 percent) have already diminished the capacity of the best of our institutions to serve the nation.

Few if any of the social, economic, technological, and political problems that the United States and the rest of the world confront in looking forward to the future will be solved directly in the major research universities. If this is true, does it matter that they are eroding and may become less effective? Why not let them gradually find their places or even disappear in a system dominated by an emphasis on equality? The oversimplified answer is that whatever hopes exist for mankind are slimmer without the vision, ferment, exploration, and occasional discovery nurtured in places like the University of California at Berkeley and the University of Chicago. The coming together of intellects who see the world and the human experience from a variety of perspectives creates an institution and an atmosphere that society seems unable to sustain in any other form than the research university. The think tank, the problem-solving institute, the specialized consulting firm, and other modern inventions for encouraging the endeavors of the few people who know a very great deal about something—all of these have their uses. But the natural home of the scholar and teacher remains the university, with its traditions of free inquiry and exploration of the unknown. Only the university creates new generations of scholars, and its atmosphere appears better designed than any other to fertilize the unfettered speculation that may often seem impractical and useless in its origins but may lead to very great breakthroughs both in science and in humanity's perception of itself.

So while we cannot draw a direct line of cause and effect between what happens to universities and our capacity to solve our day-to-day problems, it is fair to argue that our great universities are in many respects the basic source of capital upon which much of what is done by the more practical agencies in society ultimately depends. Their training and research activities undergird in subtle ways the quality of what is done at other and less prestigious institutions and simultaneously offer reference points and standards for scholarly integrity that reach outside the realm of higher education and into the world of affairs.

These observations argue for a more conscious approach than

this nation has had in its public policies to the maintenance of a limited number of absolutely first-class institutions, universities that harbor in their academic departments and professional schools a considerable proportion of those men and women judged by their scholarly peers to excel, and that maintain also the extensive libraries and laboratories needed for work of the finest quality. Some of these select (elitist, if you will) institutions come from our tradition of state-supported institutions; others reflect the tradition of private higher education. Over the next 25 years we must apply our inventiveness to the ways by which 15 to 20 major research universities can emerge as standard bearers.

The means to a more conscious national policy toward our major universities will not be easy to find: Political forces are better adapted to spreading educational benefits than to concentrating them. It would in any case be foolhardy to try to foresee all the elements on which such a policy might be built. The implications of such a policy reach to state government as well as to the federal government. Restricting my comment only to the latter, here are some possibilities to consider:

Major federal support for the large, comprehensive research libraries of the country both in and out of universities, with leadership taken by the Library of Congress. Research universities now find their libraries impossibly expensive and absolutely necessary. A program of assistance to help run libraries more effectively and cooperatively would do much for the universities.

Introduction of a system that would allow major research universities to plan ahead for five years for most of their federal support. Dozens of federal agencies and programs now turn their money on and off like water faucets through annual appropriations. No one in the federal government worries about the research universities as institutions. The result is a sporadic flow of federal funds responsive to the short-term goals of government agencies and unresponsive to the health of universities that may draw as much as 50 percent of their annual budgets from the national government. University leaders are understandably wary of the heavy hand of government in their affairs—they have experienced everything from unconstructive loyalty oaths to picayune bureaucratic meddling in their affairs—so they resist suggestions patterned on the British University Grants Commission and other models. But somehow we must find the way to channel student support, research support, and other program support so that those responsible for the fortunes of these precious institutions are not at the yearly mercy of executive departments and appropriations subcommittees that sometimes deal unpredictably with policy on the basis of whimsy. Witness the recent fiasco of the National Science Foundation with its long tradition of responsibility and integrity finding its total discretion and judgment questioned because of a single controversial action. Particularly in the area of research support there is a current tendency to starve basic research in favor of immediate payoffs from applied research. The United States spent less in 1976 on scientific research and development than it did a decade before. Both our economy and our security will suffer from this neglect in the 1980s.

A basic national program for the development of the best talent in the country in all fields of learning—sciences, social sciences, humanities, and arts. We have had bits and pieces of such a system but never a comprehensive approach to it. When the Woodrow Wilson Fellowships were at their peak, they provided an important component of such a system on a private basis. The National Science Foundation fellowships and other federal programs have helped to meet this need. But all these efforts have had the aforementioned characteristic of annual adjustments based either on the goals of particular programs or on short-range manpower projections. What is required is a basic, large-scale system of graduate and postdoctoral fellowships awarded competitively to students of the greatest promise who will select their own institutions. Each fellowship must be accompanied by an institutional grant that accurately reflects the real costs of education. This entire system should be set up so that it has long-term funding and so that adjustments are planned several years ahead. It will serve us better if it can be operated by an agency that has some protection from political pressures. If the United States is able to create a Federal Reserve System to guard its fiscal integrity, perhaps it can devise analogous arrangements for its intellectual resources.

An improved federal commitment to the support of international studies. Our country's effort to deal sensibly with the situation in Vietnam was seriously handicapped by our lack of persons who knew anything about Vietnam history, culture, and traditions. We need people who know about China, about the Middle East, about the new and the old nations of Africa in all their ramifications, just as we need authorities on the economy, politics, and defense systems of the Soviet Union. As an interdependent world evolves economically and politically, we shall need many more such people. They cannot be created overnight on the basis of sudden demand in a crisis. The professoriat to train them and the special library collections to build their knowledge have to be maintained year in and year out. The government has been relatively unresponsive to this requirement in both its executive and legislative branches.

Attention to these initiatives during the coming years would help to preserve the elements of excellence in our diverse postsecondary education system. At the same time we must pay attention to the issues of equality. We must continue to attack unfairness and discrimination in educational opportunity based on the illegal criteria of race or sex. And we must make sure that the economic circumstances of individuals and families have as little influence as possible on their chances for obtaining the benefits of advanced learning.

There has been steady, slow progress on these fronts in recent years, but there is a long way to go before blacks, Mexican Americans, Puerto Ricans, and Native Americans, to name the most underrepresented in higher education, get a fair share of educational opportunity in the United States. The legal pressures and fiscal programs that have stood behind the progress of the last 20 years will have to be continued, and the last quarter of this century will see a time when that is not easy to do. In a sense, these equality issues in higher education tend to lose their appeal. New and more strident causes emerge and get priority attention; claims are made that progress is adequate (which is not true); the first enthusiasm of a movement for equality wanes as it settles into a long and difficult war instead of the quick campaign some had anticipated; and problems emerge because mere access to opportunity is clearly not enough to overcome the complex effects of a hundred years of discrimination. The fact is that this country in mid-century began revising its treatment of many of its people. We will be lucky to have completed that task by the year 2000, but we must stick to it.

In the course of the next 25 years, we need some new initiatives in the name of equality. One that has great appeal is the creation of a so-called "entitlement" for every person in the United States. In effect this would be an educational drawing account for postsecondary education services that each person received from the federal government as a birthright and that would continue throughout life. Each of us might be given the right to two years of advanced education to use in any way at any time. It could start in college at age 19 or in law school at age 38; it could lead to vocational or professional improvement or simply to wider horizons of interest and appreciation; it would be available to every person regardless of income or need. For those who did not choose to use its benefits during their working years, it would still be available during retirement, or it could be surrendered at retirement for a bonus in Social Security payments. Some such system is the logical extension of two powerful movements now afoot in postsecondary education: the rapid expansion of flexible education services to older age groups; and the growing role of the federal government in both Democratic and Republican administrations since 1960 in providing a major component of student support at both private and public colleges and universities. This federal role is seldom seen in its entirety by anyone except officials of the Office of Management and Budget, who are aware that the combination of payments under the Veterans Administration, Social Security Administration, Basic Opportunity Grants Program, Guaranteed Student Loan Program, and other programs too numerous to mention adds up to a very large annual contribution to the cost of postsecondary education. The financial implications of a two-year entitlement may be smaller than we think if its design is rationalized with these programs to avoid duplication.

Returning to the argument at the beginning of this essay, it is important to reiterate that the shifts in style, emphasis, content, and method that will come in postsecondary education in the next 25 years will be worked out primarily at individual institutions. These are the stuff of education itself and are not appropriate matters for government attention. They are the daily business of professors and students and deans and sometimes of presidents, who must be free both to try new directions and to perpetuate what they find valuable. Given the freedom they ought to have, they will produce in the next century a diversity more interesting than today's.

For All and for Each

K. Patricia Cross

For the past 100 years it has been fairly safe to predict the continued growth of almost everything in higher education. But strange things are happening in this once predictable world. Recently, the forecasters of college enrollment had to return to their charts when the percentage of male high school graduates entering college dropped off sharply instead of continuing its steady climb. That new trend, combined with a declining birthrate, led to what almost everyone regarded as a somber warning of a no-growth future. But no sooner had the phrase "steady state" worked its way into the language than enrollment forecasters began snatching back their gloomy statistics to incorporate the unpredictable rise of adult college enrollments into their forecasts. Seemingly, the world of higher education has become less predictable; either people are behaving in whimsical ways, or we need a new model for thinking about the future.

Perhaps education has outgrown the two-dimensional charts. Extrapolations that assume the extension of the past have reached the asymptote in some cases and the point of practical absurdity in others. It is hard, for example, to think of any segment of the population that has not now been considered in the trend toward the democratization of higher education. It is hardly prophetic to suggest that within the next 25 years, colleges will be serving ethnic minorities, poor people, women, senior citizens, part-time learners, prisoners, low achievers, and anyone else who wants to be served. We will simply run out of groups to include in the egalitarian thrust that has been the major force for change throughout the history of higher education in this country.

Not only are we running out of enrollment trends, but it looks as though we shall do so without solving some of the problems we thought we were addressing. Although universal education has certainly raised the floor of learning in this country, it is difficult to demonstrate that we are making substantial progress in bringing about equality through education. Indeed, there is some evidence that the disparity between the "haves" and "have nots" has not grown appreciably less with our increased efforts to provide universal access to college.

The social inequities that propel egalitarianism are far from resolved, and the drive for equality through education will no doubt continue to be a compelling force for change in higher education. But these problems can no longer be addressed through quantitative changes—more degrees for more people; they will have to be approached through changes in the kind of education offered. We shall need new models to deal with new kinds of change.

The expansion of the curriculum has followed essentially the same pattern as the growth in enrollments. As enrollments grew by including new segments of the population, so curricula expanded by adding new fields of study. The land-grant movement expanded the classical curriculum to include applied subjects, and community colleges expanded the interpretation of "applied" to include vocational subjects. Now people are talking about expanding the curriculum to include avocational subjects.

The problems of the bloated curriculum have been exacerbated by the explosion of knowledge within each course of study. Instead of academic disciplines fragmented only to the point where experimental psychologists share no common vocabulary with which to converse with clinical psychologists, we are rapidly approaching the point where the sub-branches of clinical psychology have almost nothing in common. Libraries are moving from shelving bulky books to storing microfilm to pondering a new technological version of the old philosophical question, How many books can be stored on the head of a pin?

The ultimate extrapolation of an educational model that aims to pass along the heritage of human knowledge in the form of subject matter content is rapidly reaching the point of practical absurdity. It is ridiculous to attempt to identify *the* common core of subject matter that should be known by a college graduate, and it is increasingly difficult even to agree upon a common core within disciplines. In much the same way that we seem to have reached the end of groups of people that can be included in higher education, we seem to have reached the practical end of the content that can be added to the curriculum. Furthermore, the trend toward curricular expansion, like the egalitarian trend, has left unsolved educational problems in its wake. There is no indication that the easy availability of knowledge has resulted in generations of young people who know more than those of the past. In fact, if nationally standardized tests are a measure of knowledge, all indications are that recent high school graduates know less than those of a decade ago.

These examples of trends for the two major components of higher education—students and subject matter—illustrate the need for new models that are less dependent on extrapolation to provide a glimpse of the future. Reliance on trends and prediction formulas cranked out by computers and technicians will be of limited usefulness in twenty-first-century education. We will need models that can handle qualitative, as well as quantitative, change.

I believe that planning models for the future will be bolder, involving relatively more emphasis on direction by educational statesmen and somewhat less reliance on prediction by technicians. Instead of permitting what has happened or is happening to predict the future, twenty-first-century educators will give more attention to problem-solving models that ask what should happen. What should happen in the twenty-first century to implement the ideal of quality education for all people? And what should we teach in our colleges?

The deepest problems of egalitarian ideals cannot be addressed by simple growth formulas. Equality is a relative concept, and the "haves" always seem to have a running head start on the "have nots." I doubt that we will narrow the opportunity gap by continuing to provide the "have nots" with what the "haves" had two generations ago. They will just never catch up. To cite but one example, by the time the "have nots" from poor rural areas got to the "good life" of the cities, the "haves" in the cities had fled to the "good life" of the suburbs. Likewise, now that the "have nots" are finally getting college degrees, the commercial value of the certificate is becoming deflated, and people are questioning the nation's ability to support large numbers of college graduates in the style to which they have become accustomed. In short, the old growth model has outlived its usefulness. Equality will not be attained through simple numerical approaches, nor will educated people be produced by stuffing minds with subject-matter content.

The model that will gradually replace the growth model during the remaining years of this century is a pedagogical model that concerns itself with how education can maximize the potential of the individual. Education for all was a twentieth-century goal;

education for each will be the major goal of the twenty-first century. The components of the new model are already in place: individualized instruction through self-pacing, individually designed learning contracts, personalized systems of instruction, personal growth groups. Such programs are concerned with pedagogy and individual development through learning, and they are different in kind from the issues of access to college that dominate today's equal opportunity programs. Ironically, we are discovering that mass education is not the inevitable route to education for the masses. The very diversity of the masses calls for the abandonment of mass approaches that assume students can be batched in groups and processed through a standard pipeline designed for some mythical average student.

But isn't individualization too costly in these days of educational austerity? Probably not. It would be hard to devise a more inefficient and costly approach to instruction than the traditional content-saturated lecture delivered to a group of 30 students who are attempting, with varying degrees of success, to take amateurish notes on information that was better presented in the textbook. Students might better assimilate information independently at their own pace; they might better use the group for the discussion of issues, and a computer for the recitation of facts; and the professor might better use the lecture to inspire through a carefully prepared demonstration of a scholarly mind at work.

The pedagogical models of the twenty-first century will use a rich variety of teaching strategies for what each can accomplish. Learning for the individual will be the measure of education, and it will not be long before we can demonstrate that individualization is more cost-effective than the mass approaches that aim for the center but miss most of the target.

In much the same way that the simple addition of more class sections to accommodate more students has failed to address the problems of educational opportunity, so the addition of more courses to accommodate more knowledge will fail to address the problems of the knowledge explosion. The old aims of providing an education that can last a lifetime are gone forever. Any type of vocational or professional knowledge is quickly outdated, and even education that is pursued for personal satisfaction and the enrichment of life changes with the times and with the developing individual. P. Blake, a well-known architect, wrote in *The Atlantic Monthly* (September 1974) that "...almost nothing that we were taught by our betters in or out of the architecture schools of the mid-century has stood the test of time. Nothing—or almost nothing—turns out to have been entirely true." If knowledge is tentative in such an empirically demanding field as architecture, consider the problems of the social sciences. Donald Campbell, president of the prestigious American Psychological Association, who has looked at the past and probable future of some realms of psychology, recently urged his colleagues to teach so as to remove "any arrogant scientistic certainty that psychology's current beliefs are the final truth...." The new humility that is making its appearance in some academic disciplines is giving impetus to the search for models of teaching that move away from the teacher as purveyor of subject matter.

It has been said that education is what remains after content has been forgotten. Most learned people who use their minds as active tools rather than storage tanks would agree. To be sure, students cannot learn to think in the absence of something to think about, but the content-heavy undergraduate curriculum is already in danger of sacrificing education to the mere accumulation of quickly outdated information. The teacher of the twenty-first century will be concerned with the development of the intellectual resources of students. The move will be away from teaching content as an end, and toward using it as a means to the cultivation of intellectual skills.

If the pedagogical model is lurking just around the corner, then both administrative and academic power brokers have something to worry about. Passing from the scene is the all-consuming concern about growth that built the administrative machines of education; going, too, is the arrogance of disciplinary specialists who enter college classrooms proud of their disdain for pedagogy. Higher education will be primarily concerned with developing the capacity of each human mind to cope with a wide array of problems—personal and societal, as well as academic.

IV
In Pursuit of the Millennium

Taking the Helm

Frank Newman

On all sides, the problems for higher education seem to have become subtler, more difficult, more intractable. My own concern is whether, in growing so large so fast and with so little attention to organization and management, we may have created inadvertent forces for regulation and bureaucracy that may overtake us within the next quarter century. Can we find the will and the organizational methods to preserve autonomy, flexibility, and differentiation in higher education? Will the whole process of multicampus systems and 1202 commissions; federal and state regulations; unions and systemwide personnel practices; teaching load requirements and cost per full-time equivalent student; affirmative action and grievance procedures; lawyers and courts; budget reviews and budget re-reviews; WICHE systems to standardize terminology, accounting practices, and ranks and serial numbers; will all of this simply drive us out of the education business and into the bureaucracy business?

Are we headed toward that excess of red tape and routine in which the essential fact is that less and less gets done, and the essential response is to look out for oneself? There are certainly models for this kind of behavior: the city government of New York, for example, or the economy of Great Britain, or—all too close to higher education—large city school districts such as those in Philadelphia, Detroit, and San Francisco. If we are not careful, much of the life of the mind and the pursuit of truth will disappear—and not because of political repression, against which academic defenses are always on the alert. Rather they will be smothered to death, bit by bit, while we look the other way.

Much of this frustrating ooze of bureaucracy has been caused by the tendency within higher education and the government agencies with which it deals to underestimate the complexity of the educational and social problems we are addressing. Serious analytical thinking about how these problems should be approached is needed, but the tendency instead has been to depend too heavily on two techniques that seem to promise quick results: spending to solve some problems, and regulation to ensure compliance in the solution of others. Once we have identified a problem—the need for better education of the disadvantaged, say, or the small percentage of faculty and administrative positions held by women and minorities, or the capacity of most students to communicate or to comprehend mathematics—the response has been to convince the college or university administration (or the state or federal government) either to (a) provide new programmatic funding, or (b) devise a regulation making the appropriate practice compulsory. And for some problems, these techniques may be appropriate. The former worked well in expanding the number of classrooms and laboratories and libraries during the fifties and sixties; the latter in ending the kind of overt racial discrimination that barred James Meredith at the university door.

But neither technique has helped increase, or even measure, the impact of higher education on its students. Neither has helped most students to write decently. It has proved easier to publish affirmative action regulations than to improve the actual balance of minorities and women on faculties. It has been easier to increase the number of books in the libraries than the number of excited students reading them. No sensible approach for achieving true educational opportunity for the disadvantaged has yet proved effective.

Higher education, of course, is hardly alone. Despite endless spending and regulation, cities seem less safe than ever. No workable program for low-cost housing has been designed. Improvement in health care is noticeable, but hardly commensurate with the enormous growth in health expenditures. And despite the funding of many new programs and the imposition of endless requirements of one sort or another in elementary and secondary education, the intellectual capacity of our high school graduates seems to be declining year by year.

This failure to achieve workable and visible solutions to a host of higher education's problems has had its consequences. For one, funding has become problematic. Both legislators and the public have become increasingly skeptical that ever larger investments in higher education will in fact pay off. For another, it has become apparent that frequent recourse to regulatory methods has created a growing conflict between the desire to solve educational and social problems and the need to preserve individual and institutional freedom. If we do not wish to retreat from either of these goals, then we need more imaginative and more workable approaches to the practice of administration—not only within colleges and universities but also within those agencies that administer educational programs and systems. Unless we find more effective ways to organize our efforts, we may find ourselves in an unpleasant spiral: The difficulty of the problems and consequent slow pace in reaching solutions leads to growing frustration, which in turn leads to more regulation and directive administration, which in turn leads to less effectiveness and greater frustration, ad nauseam.

If colleges and universities are to retain collegiality, if they are to preserve the flexibility and self-determination so essential to the successful teacher or the effective researcher or the excited learner and yet still be accountable to society, then we need to reexamine the current trends in academic administration. We need to ask whether we have developed a sophistication and skill in administration to match the subtlety of our problems; whether the incentives for individuals match the needs of the institutions. If we are to be different from so much of the public service sector of society—where accomplishments have failed to match expectations— then we must go through the struggle of thinking through not only what we are doing and why, but specifically how we are going to do things.

We might begin by asking how the next 25 years will differ from the past 25. Although the economy will probably grow steadily, competition for the resources that might otherwise be used to support higher education will be tougher than ever, and it will come particularly from those public service sectors that are now large, essentially open-ended in their demands, and far less effectively managed than higher education: welfare, health care, and the preservation of law and order to name a few. Since few new approaches to these fields seem imminent, they are likely to grow steadily less efficient and will tend to absorb almost all of the new resources as they become available. Add to these the growing host of social commitments identified over the past 25 years but not yet well funded—low-cost housing, pollution control, rebuilding the inner cities—and it is apparent that competition for the social-service dollar will be intense. We cannot continue to assume that higher education will receive whatever resources it claims are needed.

Public expectations with regard to the material benefits of higher education are also certain to change considerably. For the next five years or so there will continue to be an oversupply and/or underemployment of college graduates in traditionally perceived terms. It is not that good jobs, whether in absolute numbers or as a share of all jobs, are drying up; quite the contrary. Between 1950 and 1970, good jobs (mainly the census categories of professional, technical, and managerial) have been increasing roughly at the rate of 3 percent a decade. But the rate of college going during the same period has expanded even faster, roughly at a rate of 15 percent a decade. The obvious result is that a college degree no longer guarantees one a good job. In addition, there are two less obvious consequences. College graduates are spreading out through a wider range of jobs, steadily transforming our perception of what is an appropriate occupation for a college graduate; and graduates are competing for desirable jobs with each other, transforming our perception of who gets what job and why.

These changes, on balance, are much to the good. College is still the pathway to upward mobility for many, but now to downward mobility for some. The difference is less a function of grades or selectivity of alma mater as much as of the almost forgotten virtues of motivation, ability to achieve, and imagination. College is becoming the avenue for more of the population to a wider spectrum of careers, but it no longer guarantees a sinecure. Educators must therefore end their self-inflicted dependence on the absurd argument that the prime purpose of a college education is to ensure higher lifetime earnings—an argument that has always been flawed with logical errors. We should turn instead to the argument that a sound education and the intellectual and social development of the individual are appropriate preparation for any life and any career. One would hope that this argument will force each college and university to question whether it is in fact providing such an education to its students.

These conditions are not likely to persist unchanged until the year 2000. During the past 25 years, the economy has had to absorb huge numbers of new entrants to the job market, primarily from two sources: the increase in new 18-year-olds, and the even larger numbers of married women who have decided to work. The rising aspirations of these two groups and the shift in immigration regulations to require greater professional skills for immigrants have created an intense competition for the better jobs in society.

But these pressures are bound to ease. By 1980, the number of new 18-year-olds will begin to decline. At about the same time, the flood of married women entering the labor market should stabilize since a high percentage (already about 60 percent) will already be working by then. Given any growth in the American economy, by the time society has accepted the idea that policemen and sales clerks and construction superintendents should have a college education, there will be a smaller flow of entrants into the work force.

What this will all mean is hard to tell. After all, most of the college freshmen in the year 2000 are still less than 7 years old. But surely the dynamics will be very different. Our expectation of what careers are appropriate for college graduates will be broader, but the number of new entrants to the labor market should be shrinking. My guess is that that will provide a new period of opportunity for college graduates and a strong interest in recurrent education. Many of those who have been underemployed in the current period, many women who entered the labor force in less demanding positions, and many of those concerned about either improving their education or altering their careers are likely to be interested in entering or returning to college.

Between now and the year 2000 there is also likely to be continuing pressure for accountability. In part this is a new phenomenon now demanded of all institutions—oil companies, the medical profession, even the White House. But there are special pressures on higher education. If we cannot guarantee jobs for all of our graduates, if there are not enough resources to meet the demands for social services, if the cost of attending college continues to increase, then boards of trustees and regents, legislatures and federal agencies, parents and students are going to ask some tough questions about what higher education is accomplishing. If it costs a small fortune and does not guarantee a place in the sun, what is its value? In the past we relied on a broadly shared acceptance of the intrinsic worth of higher education. Now the cost to society and the cost to the individual are high, and the automatic assumption of personal and societal benefit is being called into question. Higher education will have to argue the case for support.

Finally, we are headed toward a quarter century of legalisms, again a microcosm of similar pressures affecting all of society and partly our own fault, since we are the ones who turned out all of those lawyers in the first place. The adjustment will be particularly difficult, however, because until the middle 1960s, higher education was protected by the concept of the ivory tower from much of the regulation that affected the rest of the world. It was somehow considered different when it came to such things as unemployment compensation or collective bargaining. Those exemptions are now gone. Even the courts have ended their reluctance to interfere and are willing to consider questions of admissions, faculty promotions, student records, and so on. While most of this has been related to the essential task of protecting disadvantaged individuals, one of the unanticipated side effects has been the steady growth of procedural wrangling. The danger grows that nothing will ever be finalized; that we will come to concentrate on what is legally safe, not what is educationally sound.

These are at least some of the changes that may influence higher education between now and the year 2000; others will surely emerge. But what implications for the administration of higher education do these trends hold? There are, I believe, two distinct choices: (1) that it will become gradually more bureaucratic and meekly accept its fate; or (2) that it will try to create a different kind of administrative structure that is both workable and responsive to the new environment. If the choice is the latter, then what elements should it comprise?

In a period when institutions of higher education will probably be struggling with tight budgets requiring difficult choices among programs, with powerful external forces tending to erode institutional autonomy, and with a new level of competition among institutions for resources and students, strong leadership will be needed. Gone are the days when the ideal of a presidential search committee could be to find a pleasant soul of distinguished appearance who would offend no one. At the same time there is an increasing desire in all segments of higher education to participate in the process of governance. It is not difficult to imagine these two demands in increasing opposition to one another—a growing conflict between strong leaders and determined interest groups. The solution, I think, lies in further adaptation and refinement of the governance model that higher education has borrowed in part from American political life—a strong executive coupled with a regularized system of checks and balances.

For this to be more than just a theory, the representative bodies on campus must be streamlined. Too often faculty senates, policy committees, and student governments are ineffective, bogged down in endless debates over irrelevant issues. Yet in some institutions they play a vital role. We need to define more clearly what tasks are expected of the administration and of each of these bodies, ensuring that the governance system allows and encourages real, not just symbolic, participation in the setting of policies and priorities.

American colleges and universities might learn a good deal by studying the current trends in the administration of their European counterparts, which seem to be moving in quite a different direction. European universities have traditionally been dominated by

the relatively small number of senior faculty occupying the pro-
fessorial chairs who in turn have elected one of their number as
rector. As the demand for higher education in Europe has grown,
this method of governance has come to be seen as overly elitist and
unresponsive. In country after country, the ministry of education
has taken direct administrative or legislative action to reconstruct
the nature of university governance, often substituting some form
of committee rule. The result has been a tendency toward politicization of the university, weak institutional leadership, and a
steady shift of power, including power over the curriculum, to the
ministry.

The American approach, with its tradition of institutional identity and autonomy, is far more likely to encourage diversity, efficiency, and the conditions necessary for excitement in learning
and research. However, it requires capable leaders at all levels. We
tend to focus too much on and expect too much of the office of the
president. It is not simply a matter of work load or of sharing
blame. It is simply that we cannot have successful organizations of
the size, scope, and complexity of a modern college or university
without skilled and able administration by faculty officers, student officers, department chairmen, deans, and vice presidents—
not just by a president with an overactive thyroid.

Another step we can take toward saner administration of our affairs would be to stop pretending that we are not much concerned
about management and management techniques and begin devot-
ing some serious and sustained thinking to improving what we are
doing. We are long overdue in beginning to apply new concepts to
our own organizations that many faculty have helped to apply to
other organizations—in organization theory, management development, and many others. We must lose that studied indifference
to the practice of administration that allows us—like the British
administrators of old—to say to our colleagues that we are really
scholars and only doing this administration thing because, after
all, someone must. In some departments, the chairmanship is
passed around like a diseased beanbag. The art of administration
is difficult enough without that burden. We must be willing to face
the fact that we are administering large, complex, and important
organizations, and utilize all of the available knowledge about the
art of management.

For the first two decades of the postwar period American higher
education was decentralizing. Departments were becoming more
autonomous, a trend reinforced by the availability of outside research funding. Institutions themselves were gaining in autonomy
as well. Religious colleges, for example, loosened the bonds to

their sponsoring churches, and institutions in general became somewhat more self-directed.

But in recent years a reversal has occurred: a pronounced trend toward centralization of power. Within colleges and universities the reversal has been quite abrupt, forced at first by the need to deal with student confrontations, and later by the dilemmas of budget deficits. Simultaneously, the institutions themselves saw power devolving to outside agencies designed to supervise the colleges and universities. For many public institutions, this meant the headquarters of a multicampus system (which had grown up in most states as a means of dealing with the growing numbers of institutions). For both public and private institutions, the new statewide postsecondary commissions, designed to ensure a greater voice in the management of higher education by the public and its elected representatives, loomed on the horizon. Both of these organizational entities have begun raising questions that are new and awkward in the academic world: What is the justification for overlapping or duplicative programs; what can be done to improve the productivity of the faculty; how well is new research information being applied to current societal problems?

The common assumption has been, both on the individual campus and within the system, that we must choose between centralization and decentralization. Here again we tend to perceive this simplistically as a necessary choice between two clear alternatives. We should instead be asking which functions should be centralized and which decentralized. One reason this question has been so little asked is that most of the attention has been focused on issues of authority: Who has the right to make what decisions? Yet more important is the issue of initiative: Who is to take the initiative and leadership in a given area? What initiatives then should be decentralized?

Much of the requirement for subtlety in the management of higher education derives from the fact that the basic unit of organization is the individual faculty member in his laboratory or classroom, or from the individual student as a learner. A faculty should not be compared with a business sales force. It should not even be compared with a symphony orchestra, with many people playing individual instruments to produce a common performance. If we want advanced research, creative and effective teaching, and useful public service, then the initiative for designing and administering these programs must be decentralized to the faculty, department chairmen, and deans. Successful programs require an opportunity for those running them to use imagination and choose their own methods.

On the other hand, setting priorities and evaluating performance against agreed objectives must be done centrally. Few departments and few universities see their own needs as anything but the highest priority, or their performance as anything short of superb. The problem for any central body, whether the administration of a university, a multicampus system, or a statewide commission, is not to define by detailed regulations what people should be doing. The proper role is to set organizational priorities and to include interested parties in the process; to set the necessary conditions so that individuals and departments (or institutions) are moved to take the necessary initiative themselves in approaching their own idiosyncratic work; and to establish a means for evaluating performance.

When one examines the effectiveness of various strategies for administration, it becomes apparent that several of them have been overworked—applied to circumstances beyond their capacity. Spending money is one such strategy. But spending alone cannot guarantee results. In many of the most difficult problems we face in higher education—such as improving undergraduate education—how we proceed is more important than how much we have to spend. Major new funding resources are not likely to be available in any case.

Regulation has also been overutilized as a strategy. We should have learned—from the attempts to regulate affirmative action, to legislate campus productivity, to administer staffing by preset formulas, or to control programs by line item budgeting—that most attempts at detailed regulation of the academic process do little good and much harm.

A third overworked strategy is exhortation. Emphasis on teaching will not proceed from mere demands that the faculty give it high priority, especially when all real rewards favor time spent in research and publication.

It is not that spending, regulation, and exhortation are never appropriate as management tools, it is that they are not always appropriate. They need to be supplemented by additional and more imaginative administrative strategies. If the post office had its budget increased again, or if one more postal regulation were issued, or if Congress added red tape to the other obstructions of snow, rain, sleet, and dark of night that are not permitted to interfere with things, would it stem the continuing drop in productivity or reverse the trend toward slower delivery of the mails?

One strategy that we might adapt more widely is the use of the competitive proposal peer-review grant system that has proved effective in federally sponsored research. In the last few years, the federal government has begun to use this strategy to support new approaches in teaching and learning as well as in research. A recent study listed over 50 cases where statewide agencies or multicampus systems have used competitive grant systems in specific areas rather than simply assigning so much funding to the problem or attempting to mandate creation of programs. Several universities—MIT and the University of Rhode Island, for example—have begun to use competitive grant systems internally for student research projects, new teaching projects, and allocation of some of the funding allotted to campus maintenance and beautification. The value of a properly administered competitive grant system is that it allows the central agency to have real power over broad priorities and to alter those over time, without the resistance to change that accompanies conventional funding procedures. At the same time it does not provide control over daily operations but instead decentralizes both the design of the project and the management of its progress.

Another strategy worth attention is rethinking the reward system influencing those in higher education. We should not expect altruistic behavior of faculty, staff, or students just because they are at an institution of higher learning. For example, the advent of federally sponsored research in the postwar period reinforced the concept of publish or perish by providing a variety of financial and psychic benefits to the successful faculty researcher, including the opportunity for private funding and travel, to be consulted, and even to have better secretarial service. Can we not do more for teaching by leaving the reward for research in place but working to create an equally effective reward structure for innovative and effective teachers?

The passage of time is the enemy of flexibility in public service organizations. The older they become, the more barnacle encrusted and difficult to change they are. Now while there is still a good chance of success, higher education ought to consider a good bureaucratic housecleaning. Federal and state government agencies, postsecondary commissions, and multicampus systems ought to reexamine the growing thicket of rules and throw out the unnecessary. Educational associations could perform an important service by lobbying for codification and simplification. I do not mean here the elimination of those unpopular but important regulations that effectively serve important public purposes. I mean cleaning out the overly complicated budget procedures, the counterproductive attempts at administration from above, and the obsolete requirements from bygone eras. Institutions could do themselves a favor by improving their own procedures, by streamlining their committee structures, by eliminating outmoded practices and institutional rules. Unnecessary regulations are not neutral. Ineffective administrators hide behind them, and effective administrators are frustrated by them.

American higher education has had a long and proud history. The future, as far as one can determine, looks arduous but exciting. The very pressures and challenges of the times are likely to create incentives for reform and excellence. The one cloud growing on the horizon is the steady bureaucratization of higher education. This stifling blanket is not some evil scheme conceived by grasping bureaucrats. It is rather a natural trend resulting from size, age, and current social pressures. It is not, however, an inevitable trend. If we think about what we are doing, we can affect the evolution of academic administration. We can create a method of organization in which both creativity and accountability flourish. While no one change will achieve this, many carefully analyzed steps can make a profound difference.

We must not simply accept what is now happening in academic administration as unavoidable. If we wish to be masters of our own fate, we must have the willingness to invest our energies in analysis, discussion, and experimentation; and we must have the imagination to create management systems that encourage strong leadership and broad participation.

The Promise
of Lifelong Learning

Edmund J. Gleazer, Jr.

The theme of the 1955 convention of the American Association of Junior Colleges was "What are you doing about the oncoming tide of students?" The theme had been adapted from a widely distributed publication of the United States Chamber of Commerce about the oncoming wave of potential students, entitled "What Are You Doing About It?" In 1954 there were 2.4 million 16-year-olds approaching college age, but there were 3 million 11-year-olds and 3.8 million 6-year-olds who would be approaching college age during the 1960s. The convention was geared to inspire all states and all junior colleges to reexamine their plans and take steps to meet the needs of the oncoming and apparently ever-increasing numbers of youths in higher education.

That tide of students, the result of the baby boom following World War II, plus the effects of heightened educational aspirations made possible by the GI Bill, led to the community college boom of the 1960s. A number of national and state commissions issued reports like that of the President's Commission on National Goals in 1960: "Two-year colleges should be within commuting distance of most high school graduates...adult education should be a vital role, stressing a new emphasis on education throughout life." Another factor had come onstage: a concern not just for the 18- and 19-year-old youth and his educational opportunities but for those who were older as well.

Even those of us who were active in the field of education in the middle 1950s have almost forgotten the feverish concern aroused by the need to build as many new buildings in 20 years as had been built in the years since the nation was founded. Innumerable conferences and workshops centered on expansion of physical plant, problems of financial support, appropriate curricula, recruitment and preparation of faculty and other staff, counseling and student election, and necessary legislation, both state and federal.

Well, what happened? Was it a catastrophe? No, it wasn't. Or, it might be better to say, it hasn't resulted in catastrophe yet. Many of the necessary changes were made, the institutions expanded, hundreds of new institutions were built, both state and federal governments provided the necessary resources, and those college-age youths, most of them 18-22, were able to go to college. It was a remarkable achievement, one not sufficiently noted in our history.

But what happened to the wave? Did that big bulge on the population charts disappear after the people got through college? Or for that matter, what happened to those in that wave who didn't go to college? Those are very good questions and not often asked. No, the wave did not disappear. It still exists. And in answer to the second question, we may not know precisely where those people are who didn't go to college, but there are many of them and there is plenty of evidence that they are still out there.

Those people who were moving out of high school into college age during the seventies are now in their middle twenties. Five years from now they will be 28 to 34, and by the year 2000 most of them will still be with us and they will be in their late forties to mid-fifties. They have already entered the job market or are trying to do so. Large numbers are married. They probably have small children. They are concerned about housing. They are eligible to vote. They are making decisions. And they have educational needs.

Apparently many planners in education assumed that when these hundreds of thousands of people were suitably clothed in mortarboards and academic gowns, the case was closed as far as educational institutions were concerned. They are no longer our responsibility, we implied. They have moved into the domain of other social institutions: the unions, churches, correctional institutions, health institutions, service clubs, political organizations, hiring halls, military services, and little league. The baton has been passed. Hail and farewell. Rubbish!

Educational needs still exist for those who have moved beyond their early twenties. In fact, it would not be difficult at all to make the case that those needs may be more critical and more pressing in our society as the person moves *beyond* the conventional college age. Educational planning in our society therefore must now be based upon meeting the educational needs of the total population with an awareness of the differences that will exist in those needs at different age levels and social conditions. Sound planning cannot be limited to factors like the number of high school graduates or the number of people in what we archaically refer to as college age.

Other dramatic developments during the past decade have swollen and extended the population requiring educational services beyond high school. Among these are the strenuous efforts to increase the numbers of minority personnel having access to college, and affirmative action programs to facilitate entry into occupational fields and positions of responsibility. Another factor is sensitivity to the concerns of women, who make up over 51 percent of our total population, and of older people, whose numbers are growing more rapidly now than any other age category's.

Federal legislation has set in motion a sequence of events that results in vast needs for continuing education and training: for example, the Equal Employment Opportunity Act and the Occupational Health and Safety Act. There has been encouragement of volunteerism with its necessary education and training requirements through the Peace Corps, Urban Corps, ACTION, and thousands of other volunteer organizations ranging from the United Way to the Girl Scouts. And as a result of a fast-changing technology, the development of consumerism, and new sensitivity to public welfare, continuing education (along with licensure requirements) is mandated in a rapidly growing number of fields, either by the occupational organizations themselves or by government agencies. Consider auditing, dentistry, insurance, real estate, and the medical professions, to name but a few.

The thesis of all of this, put very simply, is that the baby boom of 20 years ago, augmented by millions of others who require and want appropriate educational opportunity in a continuing way because of many significant changes in our society, continues to have a most profound significance for educational institutions beyond high school. This fact does not appear to be sufficiently recognized at the institutional, state, or national level. We hear little discussion of the staff, facility, institutional, or financing requirements necessary to deal effectively with a wave that has assumed massive proportions from its beginning approximately 20 years ago. On the contrary, educational prophets consult the traditional stars in the conventional ways and speak of steady state and declining enrollments. Only very recently have they begun to look with some curiosity toward data that hint toward different outcomes.

The focus has been on the wrong problem. The major problem we confront in postsecondary education is not decline in the interest in education and in the need for it, but institutional and public policy changes that are essential in order to serve mounting numbers of students in times of economic constraints—a condition that promises to be long-term. What are some of these changes?

A commitment to the worth of lifelong education. Judging by the flow of literature and reports on age characteristics of students, the idea of lifelong learning, long discussed in educational circles and White House conferences, seems to be taking hold. But a kind of riptide exists between the need for lifelong education and the good sense it makes, and the apparently limited financial resources available for conventional education for traditional students. At the same time that then-Senator Walter F. Mondale proposed a "Lifetime Learning Act," community colleges in Florida expressed alarm at the possibility of having to close the "open door." A newspaper editorial proclaimed the need for priorities: "As visionary as Florida's educators and lawmakers may have been in guiding the state down a road toward lifelong education, this is an expensive trip. And when money is not available, it is necessary to proceed on a priority basis." That writer speaks for a good many state legislators and some educators. Many programs in continuing education have had to pay their own way. The policy climate has dictated the low priority given continuing education.

Lifelong learning cannot now compete with full-time undergraduate education on its own terms, but during the next 10 years this "priorities and policy" battle will be fought. By the year 2000 I would look for it to be as common for a 55-year-old to be involved in educational programs as an 18-year-old. The growing numbers and political power of an aging population will result in a reallocation of the resources directed to educational programs so that, in the words of Dean James Birren of the Leonard Davis School of Gerontology, there will be a "Graying of the University" (and of other postsecondary institutions). Community-based institutions close to people's homes—community colleges and community schools—may very well be serving as many people over 40 as under. The implications are somewhat breathtaking for course organization, teaching style, place of learning, administrative procedure (the registration line and other red tape, for example), and consumer expression.

From monolith to modules. The profound significance of a commitment to lifelong learning and lifetime education is difficult to grasp. To move in that direction means much more than some simple rearrangement of the present organization of education.

What we are talking about is revolutionary in its meaning and in its requirement for change in our institutions. Only recently has the notion been broadly accepted of universal educational opportunity through the secondary and possibly the first two postsecondary years. In the radical change necessitated I am reminded of comments made by Leonard Woodcock at the American Association of Community and Junior Colleges' convention in 1975. His remarks dealt with energy but they have a transferability to lifelong learning:

> Consider energy—the driving force of industrial societies. The size and nature of our energy problems can only be grasped when we realize that the entire structure of production and consumption in our nation is built on the assumption of cheap and abundant energy. Every factory, every machine, the location and design of every building as well as every item of consumption, has been chosen explicitly or implicitly on this assumption. Now that assumption no longer holds. That fact has been creeping up on the industrial world for some time. It burst open on October 19, 1973. It will never go away again.

Has October 19 already passed for the concept of lifelong learning? If not, when will it come? Our structures of production and consumption in education have been built on the assumption of a terminal point to education, and that assumption no longer holds. Woodcock himself describes the kind of social expectations that make it so:

> We feel—or hope—that either the time has come or must come shortly when blue-collar and white-collar workers should benefit from the opportunity to break away from the daily grind without having to walk the bricks or stand in unemployment lines; that they should be free to go back to school, or up to college, or to write a book about the life of a worker, or whatever. Such workers, we believe, need to unwind, or renew their enthusiasm, or strike out in a new direction, or improve their skills as much as any college professor.

The changes required in the "structures of production and consumption" in education are not limited to postsecondary education. There are essential interrelationships to be acknowledged and dealt with which involve postsecondary institutions, elementary and secondary education, and informal education. Postsecondary education does not signal the beginning of learning or the end of it. It is conditioned by what comes before and conditions what comes after.

The essence of the Faure report (Edgar Faure, et al., *Learning to Be*, UNESCO, 1973), with its implications for lifelong learning, can be found in its assertion that "it follows, on the one hand, that the education of children must prepare the future adult for various forms of autonomy and self-learning" and on the other hand, that "the existence and the development of many wide-ranging educational structures and cultural activities for adults, and serving their own purposes, are a precondition for reforming initial education."

By and large, college and university education has behaved as if it were the beginning and the end—a monopolistic, monolithic structure exercising power through its credentialing functions; a pyramidal form with the graduate school at the sharpened apex modifying and influencing everything below it, with the structure broadening to include larger and larger numbers toward the base. By implication those who do not reach the summit have been unsuccessful.

If education is to be lifelong, then by definition it begins very early in the game and its termination is closely linked to the individual's. The monolith no longer has any credence. In a 1970 paper on "The Learning Force," Stan Moses of the Educational Policy Research Center at Syracuse University rejected the notion that American education was a three-layer hierarchy running from primary school through graduate school. This, he said, represented the core but overlooked a periphery in which over 60 million adults pursued learning activities very important to their lives. His purpose was to challenge the monopoly the educational establishment has over public policy and public resources. Within the next 25 years, I think we will see educational systems consisting of modules with different kinds of functions serving a diversity of constituents, and with performance, not hours of academic credit, as the basis for credentials. Most important for the benefit of learners and for effective use of resources will be productive linkages among those educational institutions that have common goals and purposes. These will come either as a result of initiatives taken by educators or by legislative mandate. The handwriting is already on the wall.

Competitors or colaborers? Over the next 25 years, it is likely that among the needs given high priority in our society will be development of energy sources, mass transportation, lowered crime rates, improved and extended health services, mechanisms for dealing with air and water pollution, expanded employment opportunities, an adequate food supply, and a stabilized economy. Educators can conceive of these urgent social needs as competitors for a limited supply of dollars, and in fact they are. However, it is also possible to perceive such needs as having educational components that, if properly addressed, can in time reduce the dollar requirement for the problem area. This kind of thinking requires a community orientation. It requires continuous assessment of community change. And it involves working relationships on a continuing basis with those organizations that have planning and operational responsibilities for these varied social functions.

At the community level, I see relationships developing in constructive ways among community colleges, community schools, departments of recreation and parks, health agencies, libraries, labor unions, and volunteer organizations. In one city, a community college found that there were 300 community service agencies funded to provide services and with which the college could ally itself. In fact, community-based institutions in particular can extend their own resources by, in effect, using the budgets, the staff, and the space of other community-based organizations, including banks, department stores, and newspapers.

Cooperation among community organizations is essential but sometimes difficult. Secondary schools with shrinking enrollments are turning their attention to continuing education programs. Four-year colleges seeking additional program areas are developing more evening and extension services, and even associate degree programs. Municipal and county recreation departments have expanded adult education programs. Libraries, museums, and other agencies are also conducting community education programs. All of these efforts are welcome, but coordination and cooperation are needed. Cooperative assessment of community education needs and resources, cooperative planning of programs, and cooperative arrangements in offering and conducting services have happened in some places and can happen in others. The 1202 commissions at the state level provide a mechanism for coordination in planning, and there are some federal programs that require evidence of consultation and involvement with the interested parties. However, I would hope that by the turn of the century, local areas would have learned how to relate community agencies and organizations in educational programs within broad policy statements at the state or possibly the federal levels. Institutions that dedicate themselves to the teaching-learning enterprise ought to see the development of that capacity as a fruitful one.

"Sensing" vis-à-vis "projecting." If I were not optimistic about the future and committed to the view that we can learn to deal with our problems, I would not be in the field of education. But now I come to my greatest concern. The future is full of unknowns. Many of the old rules seem no longer to apply. The voice of the authority in a given field is often heard with skepticism, and

often speaks with equivocation. A variable like a doubling or tripling of oil prices can have the well-known domino effect on our institutions. Nevertheless, we must plan. But the institution that can deal with the uncertainties before us is the one that has a "sensing" capacity, a system of intelligence that detects significant changes in the environment and analyzes these for their meaning to the institution.

But another capacity is essential: to be able to adapt, to initiate change in the institution, to be free to act. By the year 2000 will we have learned how to keep structures flexible? Can we deal with what the Faure report calls "sociological pedantry" (arbitrary adherence to rules and forms), whether this be in the nature of collective bargaining agreements, state level legislation and administrative directives, or federal requirements? According to the December 1974 monthly letter of the Royal Bank of Canada, "Continuing education enables us to reevaluate our habits of thought, concepts, and ideals in the light of these changing times. It prepares us to face any change or chance...." The future will be a bright one if educators, too, can evidence those great benefits of lifelong learning.

Consensus and Preservation

Frederic W. Ness

J.M.:   Are you hopeful or pessimistic about the rest of the century?

A.:   I think I am both. We have it within our power, I think, *to do extraordinary things* if we want to. The question is do we want to enough? And also do we have enough— it's not merely a question of goodwill, it's a question of extreme intelligence....

—From *Aldous Huxley: A Biography*,
by Sybille Bedford

Anyone who has spent the greater part of his adult life in higher education must have been born with a predisposition toward optimism. If it survives 'until he reaches the age of acknowledged maturity, this natal impulse will have been quite vigorous indeed. As I reexamine my own brand of optimism, I should have to define it as decidedly long- rather than short-range. For the immediate future of our colleges and universities—still the most vital custodians of our culture and a principal agency for providing an enlightened citizenry—seems fairly bleak.

What is more, there is no effective way of insulating higher education and providing it with a different and more hopeful future than that of the society it serves. Without in any way denigrating its contributions, one must conclude that higher education serves but does not lead social change. It may be that the students at Nanterre in the late sixties nearly brought down the government of

France, but we could scarcely claim that the French university as an institution contributed significantly to that development. Rather, it was itself a victim of forces over which it had little or no control.

One almost has to turn to the futurists and their scenarios from the total society to make any serious predictions about the face of higher education in the coming years. Among the several of that cult whose prognostications I have reviewed, I have discovered none dispensing the kind of cheer I would welcome with my breakfast egg. For this reason I find singularly comforting an observation from that remarkable woman Françoise Giroud (in *I Give You My Word*): "Assuming that you don't confuse metaphysics with social structures, defeatism is not any more reasonable than optimism and the latter has the virtue of being bracing."

With that as a preface, I would like to review a few of the current trends shaping at least the intermediate future of our colleges and universities. The most obvious, of course, is a downward movement on the ladder of public priorities. This is no simple thing: Rather, like Jacques's melancholy, it is compounded of many simples. The campus disruptions of the sixties played a part in it. Inflation is playing a part, as is the growing suspicion that academic achievement may have only minimal relationship to success in later life, and that the financial advantages of the college degree may be fast disappearing. Certainly the increasing emphasis on other social priorities, especially health and welfare (which are rather incongruously linked with education in our federal structure), is eroding the former preeminence of higher education. And, if I dare suggest it, a certain waning of faith among the practitioners themselves, whether in the classroom or the administration building, may be having its own subtle impact.

A second important factor that will affect higher education is a diffusion, or, perhaps more accurately, a confusion, of authority. In a typical tug-of-war, the rope has two ends. In the tug-of-war going on right now in higher education, the rope is more like the spokes of an unrimmed wheel. The student movement toward participation in governance seems to be in a temporary lull (but the administrator would be well advised to remain alert). Spurred by the movement toward collective bargaining, the push for greater faculty authority over the management of the institution seems to be intensifying. At the same time governing boards, in part because of the mounting fiscal problems and in part because of more effective communication among themselves, are assuming more active responsibility for the policy and management of institutions. In the name of coordination, agencies off the campus, particularly governmental or quasi-governmental agencies, are increasingly imposing their will upon institutional administrations.

As our colleges and universities move further along the road of retrenchment, leadership may well become still more diffused. And potentially more dangerous, the decision-making level will be further removed from the scene of action. In tax-supported systems, the local administrators could become little more than branch managers.

This suggests another trend—toward consolidation and centralization. Most noticeable in the tax-supported sector, it is visible also among independent colleges and universities. There, however, it is at least voluntary, though frequently it represents a response to fiscal necessity.

One might wish to skirt the public/private issue, but the subject is too large to be overlooked. The so-called private sector is shrinking, and some observers expect it to drop to as low as 10 percent of total student enrollments. There is little meaningful support for the independent colleges from among the leaders of the tax-supported sector. And there is such a great diversity of interest within the independent sector itself that the Darwinian principle of mutual assistance within the species is likely to prove a less potent force by far than that of the survival of the fittest—in this case presumably the wealthiest and most prestigious, with a scattering of small, religiously oriented colleges. (Will this ultimately mean a private elite and a public egalitarian in our institutional pattern?)

Further, and ironically, the difference between the tax-supported and the independent sectors is becoming less clear. The mounting dependence of the independent college on the tax dollar—seemingly an essential way of life for the majority of those that will survive—will involve forms of accountability barely distinguishable from those at the so-called public institutions. At the same time, the latter seem increasingly to rely on tuition and philanthropic income. Two major research universities come to mind, the one independent, the other tax-supported. Close to 80 percent of the former's total income now comes from state and federal sources; 30 percent of the latter's derives from philanthropic sources. The most obvious difference between the two is the way in which their trustees are chosen and perceive their responsibilities.

There seems to be a lively debate at present as to whether, in their goals and processes, our colleges and universities are becoming more alike or more diverse. If we were ever to develop a system of matching the student and the institution, which is highly unlikely in our form of democracy, then diversity would be easier to sustain. In the meantime, I see a trend toward similarity in curricular offerings and forms of delivery. Experimentation, even the will for change and innovation, is likely to diminish in the intermediate future as faculty become more concerned with job security and administrators worry about institutional survival.

The largely false dichotomy between the liberal and the vocational will continue to haunt us as well. Perhaps more and more of our educational leaders will conclude that the problem is basically whether we should provide training merely for short- or for long-range need. In point of fact, we can and must do both. But here the economy will be a much more potent force than the convictions of professors or administrators. Colleges will need to attract students; students will need to qualify for jobs. Curricular trends, even in the liberal arts college, will be toward more vocational emphases and, in order to guarantee a proper mix, toward far greater prescription than has been evident in the recent past. In the long run, the students themselves may discover that an exclusively vocational curriculum can be too limiting, and they may demand a broader educational experience. I hope this occurs well before the year 2000.

Yet another trend is the partially conscious but not wholly deliberate commitment toward two distinct but related goals: universal higher education and a learning society. We seem to be moving in the direction of the former as a matter of national policy, with federal and state programs striving to provide equality of access and choice. There is even some evidence that we might slowly be approaching the latter: By a recent count, there were more part-time than full-time students enrolled in postsecondary institutions. The assumption is that a high percentage of these part timers could be loosely classified as adults and thus foreshadow the social mode of a learning society.

Accordingly, although I remain mildly skeptical, our academic institutions will no longer be concerned basically with the "rites of passage" of youth into society but will be involved in meeting a vastly wider range of social needs and personal aspirations. B. F. Skinner in *Walden II* asserted nearly three decades ago that we already possess the knowledge and skill to meet all of our physical needs without anyone's having to work more than two hours a day. The real problem may be how people can possibly use all of their free time, not necessarily for productive purposes but to avoid boredom. It is, of course, inconceivable that our colleges and universities will not be obliged to serve this kind of social need, or that this development will not have a profound impact.

Three caveats must be offered at this point. First, each person will read different trends in his crystal ball. Second, he will ascribe to them varying degrees of importance. And third, it is the essential nature of trends that they can wax or wane or, for that matter, turn into something quite different. As the philosopher Whitehead used to caution his students, "It is the business of the future to surprise us."

But if I could now discard all the preceding and walk the fine line between what may be and what I hope will be, I would envision something like this:

I would acknowledge Sir Toby Weaver's suggestions to the Organization for Economic Cooperation and Development that the experience of higher education should give students competence, comprehension, cultivation, creativity, communion, and capability. Yet I believe we must go beyond this list of objectives for the simple reason that the clientele of our institutions of higher education will have a predictable range of needs and expectations.

Weaver's goals will be most applicable (though far from exclusively) to the young adults who will still need to have their energies focused and talents directed through some formal institutional structure. And since there is evidence that the residential experience provides the most meaningful education, I would anticipate the continued existence of the campus in some form.

There is a second group, however, that will require other kinds of academic experience. These are the adults in the middle years— years of maximum social and economic productivity—who will need to make up educational deficits, undergo retraining, or pursue more intensified specialization. Again, this would seem to call for the maintenance of some form of institutionalized higher education, though not necessarily the campus as we know it.

Finally there are the older adults who have, in essence, made their contribution to society and who are now at a time when education can provide much needed enrichment and recreation. They will not be well served by a delivery system consisting primarily of a television set or a teaching machine (enormously useful devices in their place) but will be best served in an academic, possibly even a campus, setting.

In summary, I believe that we shall have, in AD 2000, as great a need for colleges and universities in as great a variety of sizes and shapes as now. But there will be some vital differences. Just as we have recently been able to divest ourselves of much of the restrictive *in loco parentis* responsibilities, the college and university of the future will be largely freed from the constraints of certification and credentialing—from the role of social selection that has so often worked against the learning process.

Our academic institutions will become true learning centers. Some will be large and comprehensive; others will be of more modest size and limited in scope. Some will serve all three generations; others will limit themselves to one or two. There will be a few centers for the elite, but not so sheltered as to remove them from the marketplace of ideas—as has been done for centuries. Since we seem to be on the edge of enormous new discoveries about the functioning of the human mind, it is impossible to predict the methodologies and processes that will be employed in these future academic settings. But the faculty will undoubtedly constitute a major learning resource, disseminating their wisdom through lectures and other forms of communication. Basically, however, the professor will be a guide and a stimulus to learning, while himself contributing to the discovery and synthesis of knowledge.

I view this future for higher education not without some grave doubts. Jefferson, on his founding of the University of Virginia, may well have envisioned a commitment "to equality of opportunity and aristocracy of achievement," a concept that, I regret to say, already seems a little simplistic. How tenable will it be in the future? The ultimate problem may be whether any future system of higher education—any array of learning centers—will be able to discover a consensus and then transmit, effectively, those values that are essential to the preservation of the society it serves. If it cannot perform this function—and some would hold that television is already a more forceful transmitter of values, however questionable, than colleges and universities—then the face of higher education in 2000 may well be reflected in a shattered mirror.

Three Reforms

Paul C. Reinert

E ducation forms and fashions society. This is theoretically
true. And at least partially true historically. But the converse
is far truer—that society forms and fashions education. What men
want and what men believe become the objectives and content of
education. Therefore, the most important questions relating to the
future face of higher education are: What will and what should
Americans want from higher education over the next several generations?

I would hope that it will be considerably different from what we
seem to have been wanting (either deliberately or subconsciously)
in recent decades. And I would hope higher education in the United
States would be different by the year 2000 because the nation
wants it different—different from now in three fundamental ways:

Objectives: goals that are openly stated and honestly believed
in; goals based upon the development of the whole human person,
on fundamental moral and spiritual values and principles, on a
recognition of the importance of man's relationship to his fellowmen.

Quality, content, and atmosphere: regarding the first, equity
for all but not through diminishment of standards or disregard for
quality and intellectual demands; concerning the second, a flexible, vitalized educational experience that imparts not only knowledge but sound qualities of mind and a wide range of interests;
with regard to the third, a much closer relationship and inter-
change between education and the family, business and the com-

munity, with less institutionalization, isolation, and compartmentalization.

Structure of the system: reconstruction of the financing system of higher education to provide reasonable economic hope for independent colleges and universities, enabling them to stand alongside their state and proprietary counterparts with a vigor and health and stability based upon national commitment to diversity and pluralism in education.

Returning to the matter of objectives, it has been said that we are living in the age of the diminishment of man. It is the role of higher education to assure that such diminishment not be our legacy to the twenty-first century. This means that higher education must define and establish a set of principles for itself. Principles that not only set forth the academic work to be done but also commit us to preparing people for more than just earning a living. These goals and principles must be determined and steadfastly adhered to in the way that our Constitution guides our government.

There is a kind of notion we're all sharing that higher education has lost its value structure. I would judge that American higher education has not become value-free and purposeless, but has sold itself to questionable values and unworthy purposes. It is shot through with such false values as the assumption that the personal character of the teacher is irrelevant in terms of his professional competence; that human personality can become "whole" through intellectual growth alone; that there are no transcendent values but only relative, ephemeral ones. In short, our inadequate definition of values has us trying to figure out which values of society most people in that society will accept. Along with our other social institutions, higher education is succumbing to the notion that the people will have their way.

Yet around us we see the unhappy product of such accommodation—for one, a new low state of public morality as it relates to the public milieu. And we ask, What went wrong?

The educational enterprise must exert strong influence if it, together with other social institutions including government and the church, is to lead us out of the wilderness of inhumanity, slackened morals, and purposelessness.

While it is important, knowledge by itself only informs. Free men with knowledge but without values are hazards, dangerous to themselves and to others. How, then, can the academic institution banish values from its sight? Yet both by custom and by law, most education in this country has become education without values, failing to supply the why of a fully human decision. Certainly this describes the situation in our secular colleges and universities.

In the practical order, there seems to be no way, for example, that a state-supported school or even a secular private school can arrive at an institutional consensus on such matters as the worth and dignity of the human being, or the role of the state in relation to the individual. Much less can they adhere to values that might be termed transcendental—that is, values that are real and objective, independent of one's own personal attitudes, preferences, or desires.

It is my belief, however, that rather suddenly, valueless education has lost much of its appeal. Church-related campuses are suddenly being perceived as relevant, exciting, important places for doing what they've always done, and I see this as reason to take heart.

But our nation does not have until the year 2000 to awaken to the critical importance of those independent institutions that provide value-based education. Or to make it possible for a much greater segment of higher education to serve a moral and civic function as well as an intellectual one. For we are a nation in transition. Ideas are being generated that will forge a new American society. We are rethinking our traditions as well as our values. Laws, attitudes, goals, expectations, and government and corporate activities are all facing harsh judgments. There will be national choices made. And it is on our campuses that intellects capable of making proper choices must be molded.

Contrary to popular warnings, we must assume responsibility for the development of the total person. Which means that we must have as our concern the discovery and evaluation of what is happening to the whole individual as he moves through the educational process, and the kind of human being that emerges from that experience.

The mission of the teacher must go beyond transmitting knowledge to interpreting the student's environment and helping him both to develop standards and to defend them. This must be accepted as a teaching responsibility, not as something relegated to the student services department to be dealt with as a psychiatric assistance or special help.

At the turn of the next century, just as now, the big experience at the college level will be maturation of what the student believes in. It is up to our teachers in the classrooms to guide him as his values change from gut feelings to rational positions and to fortify him intellectually. Concomitant with such teaching dedication should be the determination of the academic community to live out these values in the learning/teaching experience.

Turning to the question of educational quality, we have a crisis of traditions as well as conscience to resolve. It is the collision of demand for universal education with demand for educational excellence. The price paid for universal access has been a decline in the standards of our colleges and universities, though we don't like to admit it. The condition cannot be abided unless we likewise will abide a second-rate brand of education.

Even the intellectual leadership of minority groups questions whether relaxing of academic standards really is in society's interest. The noted black historian John Hope Franklin of the University of Chicago has had this to say: "We should expect our educational institutions to do more than perpetuate myths and false notions about our vaunted egalitarianism. This is not to say that once relieved of that intolerable burden they are then prepared to fulfill the great expectations of satisfying the intellectual needs of those who seek fulfillment and of our society that desperately needs their care if it is ever to become truly democratic. It is to say that whatever their function as guardians and purveyors of our intellectual traditions, our schools and colleges must be recognized as agencies for establishing and maintaining the highest standards of excellence." Many of those who have been processed automatically through our higher education system are finding that the time, work, and money invested have only admitted them to the ranks of the overqualified and the unemployed.

Certainly our educational system must recognize the diversity of human capacities and interests to be served, and certainly it must serve them equitably. However, where higher learning is concerned, the spirit of egalitarianism is more properly met by safeguarding against inequalities of opportunity within a meritocratic structure, not by assuming every high school graduate automatically eligible for and capable of obtaining a degree. Intellectual achievement cannot give way to motivation or good character as the central qualification for graduation from college.

As for educational content, what is called for is a vitalizing of liberal learning. We are going to have to teach the liberal arts in the context of living—of the real world. And while the curriculum should continue to be based upon traditional academic disciplines, the student's exposure to them should be shaped by two ingredients not sufficiently present today in many colleges: contact with professors who are deliberately interdisciplinary in their thinking and teaching; and opportunity for the content, principles, and values of liberal education to be tested and applied in life situations both on campus and off, whether through interspersed periods of off-campus experience—internships within the student's selected field—or through on-campus simulation of these situations.

The dangers of isolation and insulation must be dealt with. The condition is more prevalent in the liberal arts than in the professions and vocations. When you are teaching literature, you don't have to keep up with the outside. Thus we see some professors no longer teaching with any sense of reality.

Higher education tends to create a world of its own, and the propensity warrants concern. For when education gets so far removed that students are just looking at a picture instead of at reality, critical dimensions are lost.

To obviate the condition, liberal arts of the future must follow more closely the professional and vocational model. Disciplines such as engineering, architecture, and business administration bring both students and faculty into contact with outsiders.

Also, faculty leaves should provide time off not merely for professors to do their own thing as they do now but to pursue a program of defined objectives designed to ensure that they never lose touch. They must not become critics of something quite different than that which really exists, or a reclusive kind of leisure class, critical of the outside world and defensive of their own.

The third fundamental way I would hope higher education in the United States will be different by the year 2000 concerns its structure. At present we are drifting relentlessly toward homogenization, toward the destruction of the most precious of all characteristics of American higher education—its diversity. To continue on our present course will find us, shortly, with institutions that proffer one face, one style, one character.

A distinction must be drawn between conformity caused by a self-induced poverty of individuality on the part of the institution, and that imposed by economic pressures. Where institutions lack adequate funds they are prey to a kind of economic homogenization that dissolves the unique, melts down differences, blunts character, and brings a sameness throughout. Perhaps the greatest forfeiture of distinctiveness has been in church-related colleges and universities forced to change their structure so that they might qualify for essential types of government aid programs.

Thus a very real concern with government aid is that it be provided in the future so as not ultimately to defeat the purpose and goal of preserving diversity. Funds necessary for sustaining our system must come in a manner that accommodates constitutional restrictions on the one hand while not forcing diversified education into a homogeneous mass on the other. We must make sure that we are not left with a stereotyped educational factory.

Needed is a universally acceptable method of equalizing the economic competition between our tax-supported and independent sectors. At the very least, federal and state support needs to be provided to both sectors in accordance with a more unified, rational design: less scattering of categorical programs, for one; for another, some form of student aid similar to a voucher system that will provide everyone with access to and a choice of educational institutions based upon types of programs offered rather than economic restriction. The approach would limit any government control to a minimum while maximizing a healthy and beneficial marketplace competition among institutions. In addition to direct aid to students I see the independent sector's best hope in contractual services rather than in unrestricted grants to institutions.

I am encouraged by the pressure for statewide planning encompassing all higher educational resources. For one thing, it is the only way the public and political power structure will be made aware of the contributions, problems, and needs of the independent sector. But to keep government control in check, planning boards must be made up of laymen, not politicians. Also, the degree of state involvement can be counterbalanced by federal incentive programs and other forms of shared responsibility. The more diversified our sources of support, the less the danger of our system becoming a creature of government.

It should be our gravest concern as a nation that our higher education system not be allowed to suffer financial collapse and that its needs be approached pluralistically. We must strive together toward a healthy new financial equilibrium or such collapse is inevitable. We are fast running out of time to affect the outcome. Yet our system will need to be fiscally sturdy if it is also to be at its most responsive as both an intellectual and a moral force during the years immediately ahead.

It might be said of American higher education that its achievements have been Homeric, its agonies have been Sophoclean, and its prospects resemble the perils of Pauline. The only certainty of the moment is that, as it strives to prepare us to live our lives fully and well, it will continue to be caught between the abrasive forces of those who expect too much and those who provide too little.

Yet prevail it must. For as we enter a new age of man—in the year 2000, if not before—an age in which persons will pursue several careers successively, have far more leisure time, live with as yet unfathomable advances in technology, and confront perhaps equally unfathomable social needs and ills (some of them, perhaps, irremediable), it will be higher education that stands as the nation's last great hope. But, for that hope to be justified, we must achieve a higher education that is different in important ways from what we know today.

The Tyranny of the Urgent

Albert Quie

It is possible to be fairly optimistic, if not enthusiastic, about some of the developments in higher education in recent years. If change comes more slowly to higher education than to some organizations, there are nevertheless continuing experiments that give much promise for the future. Yet we are in the midst of profound uncertainty about our colleges and universities. There appears to be a new institutional identity crisis that, along with severe financial strain, has brought on a state of depression. We also seem to be detecting a curious public reaction to colleges as to other social institutions, namely, that as our institutions try to appease their critics by being more "responsive" and willing to bend one way or another, the level of respect for those institutions declines.

To what do we attribute the lessening impact of so many of our social institutions—schools, churches, Boy Scouts, government, universities? Why do not more Americans demonstrate pride and loyalty toward these institutions—the "best in the world," as we are so often told? Why are there so few leaders of these institutions to whom people look as models for their own lives?

The opening paragraphs of Frederick Rudolph's *The American College and University* include this observation: "At the beginning, higher education in America would be governed less by accident than by certain purpose, less by impulse than by design." Can we say today that higher education is moving with "certain purpose"? I think not. In fact, I would suggest that the crisis higher education faces is a crisis of purpose. Most of our time is devoted to questions of governance, finance, tenure, credits and degrees, admission standards, course requirements, public accountability...but to what end? Why is such an elaborate, expensive, time-consuming enterprise necessary to the life of our society?

The traditional functions of higher education have often been stated as the discovery of knowledge; the transfer of knowledge from one generation to the next; the development of trained manpower; and the education of the whole person. It might be enlightening to evaluate how well these functions are being carried out today and the extent to which our society should depend on the campus in the future.

The purpose currently enjoying the most popularity is education as preparation for work. Everyone seems to understand this and to assume that most citizens need such an education. But sociologists and economists are now challenging our public policy assumptions about the economic payoff of education to both the individual and society. We are told that many who receive vocational education could learn a job skill faster and at less expense while on the job.

Of course, as long as formal education helps some individuals earn more money, many will want it. But the social problems created by underemployment raise questions about increasing the number of college graduates beyond what the economy seems to need. Selling higher education solely on the manpower argument may turn out to be shortsighted.

In the 1600s, responsible leaders were naturally concerned about infusing culture into the rural frontier life of the colonies. Transfer of knowledge often required the aggregation of books and trained minds in one location—a campus—because these resources were few and far between. Today, with 12 years of formal learning available to all, and with modern communications and a variety of informal learning experiences, society does not feel as dependent on the campus for spreading our cultural heritage as it once did. Besides, higher education directly reaches only one third of the young adult population.

Likewise, the purpose of discovering new knowledge, which has been heavily financed through our universities during this century, is now becoming a shared purpose with many other public and private research organizations. In fact, many noncampus research efforts have as many qualified PhDs and research facilities as some of our better universities. Even though the campus remains the backbone of our nation's basic research effort, many are questioning how much money is appropriate given other needs and how many institutions should be producing doctorates.

Before turning to what I consider the most important element of institutional purpose in today's society, I would like to comment briefly on that increasingly popular function known as public service. This is a difficult function to evaluate. In one sense, all of what an institution does is in the public interest. Are there specific, unique contributions beyond the first three purposes mentioned above that society is not receiving or could not receive through a whole series of different delivery systems? Is society calling on the campus for these public service ventures, or are they often activities faculty and students determine should be provided? Are they more personally rewarding than the more demanding discipline of teaching and learning (not to discredit the legitimate claim that community service projects are often good learning experiences)? Or do campus administrators see public service projects as good public relations that might help increase the next legislative appropriations?

Although I have often applauded the many extensions of the campus into the larger community, I wonder how much we should ask or expect from our institutions of higher learning. From where has the pressure come that most institutions try to be so much to so many? Have our campuses attempted to be so responsive to all expressed needs in society that the effectiveness of their unique functions has declined?

There is a final purpose of education I have yet to discuss. The words vary, but the theme has to do with the quality of life—the discovery of oneself, a value structure for making choices, a moral standard of reference for living in a society that too often says anything goes. While this purpose is still stated in the glowing rhetoric of college catalogs and promotion brochures, too many graduates of our institutions are giving their alma maters failing grades on this score.

No individual can expect to purchase a personal ethical standard or moral identity with his tuition payment. But most surveys indicate that prospective students do expect to find an environment that encourages them in this quest for something of purpose and meaning. Knowledge alone does not guarantee happiness. Neither do the two other much sought after commodities—material wealth and social power—that many believe a college degree can help them obtain.

Why do people continue to kid themselves? Although few faculty members counsel students to seek the life worth living through money or position, many do advocate intellectual pursuits alone as the greatest good. I happen to believe the oft-stated purpose of learning for its own sake is a moral cop-out. In the eyes of many, an institution that offers nothing more than complete moral relativism has lost its reason for being.

Evidently this vagueness of purpose in the area of moral, ethical, and spiritual education was not always the condition of higher education. In commenting on the sense of mission of Harvard's founders, Rudolph explains some of their commitment:

> Intending to lead lives no less than the purest, aspiring to serve God and their fellowmen in the fullest, they acknowledged a responsibility to the future. They could not afford to leave its shaping to whim, fate, accident, indecision, incompetence, or carelessness.... A world that finds the deepest expression of its purposes and its goals in the Scriptures cannot afford to ignore the training of its Biblical expositors.

This desire to lead pure lives, to serve God and their fellowmen, and to accept responsibility for shaping the future leadership of the nation provided a strong sense of purpose for those in the colonial college. Why has the mainstream of American higher education abandoned these notions of mission? Are they out-of-date? Have we advanced beyond their relevance? I think not.

There was a time when many church-related colleges seemed not to tolerate the free and open discussion of certain issues that conflicted with denominational dogma. Today, although academic freedom has supposedly overcome this particular narrowness, many of our secular campuses find it intellectually unacceptable to discuss, for example, the relevance of Jesus Christ to one's search for meaning.

Irving Kristol, discussing the theme of moral development at an Educational Testing Service conference, observed that "liberal humanism...is the dominant spiritual and intellectual orthodoxy in America today." That is quite apparent. But what we should note and not discard before absorbing its import is Kristol's further observation:

> Though the majority of the American people may well subscribe to some version of this religion—and I think they do—they end up holding in contempt all the institutions in which the ethos of this religion is incarnated. Indeed, and incredibly enough, they become increasingly "alienated" from these institutions and end up feeling that these institutions are in some way "unresponsive" and "irrelevant" to their basic needs. And not only "unresponsive" and "irrelevant," but actually "repressive" as well. It is a historical fact of some significance, I would say, that though schools were never particularly popular institutions among

young people, it is only in recent years, as our schools have ceased trying to "form" young people and have tried instead to "develop" them, that the school has come to be widely regarded as a kind of prison.

To understand the significance of his last sentence, one needs to understand that Kristol interprets "trying to 'form' young people" as a conscious process of assisting individuals to create a moral identity, while "develop" suggests "that morality is something that exists embryonically within every child...something that happens to one." He then concludes that the moral neutrality of our institutions ends up robbing them of their popular legitimacy.

Could this explanation be a clue to why much of the public appears to be withdrawing that unquestioning enthusiasm that it injected into the bloodstream of American higher education after World War II? Further developments of the last few years that add to the force of Kristol's analysis are the popular enthusiasm for the more strictly organized parochial schools in the cities; the call for a return to the basics in the public schools; and the growth and optimism of the few dozen authentic Christian colleges.

Let me be more specific and then quite personal to make a point. Most individuals need to believe in some sort of god, meaning a belief in something that takes precedence over everything else. So the important questions are: What do I believe? How big is my god? What is the meaning of my life? Students, like everyone else, must continually ask whether their deepest need for a moral identity is being met.

I believe man was created for a purpose by a God Who revealed Himself through Jesus Christ, with Whom many enjoy a personal relationship. The ultimate purpose for living—and for learning—comes out of this belief. God created man to "have dominion over all the earth." His highest expectation for those who believe in Him is that they love one another and learn to serve their fellow man. Disciplined study, research, and the development of critical thinking then become purposeful tools for a higher goal.

Here is my point. Why are we told that such statements as I have just made are not freely shared and openly considered in the classrooms of some of our great institutions? Some students do find a sustaining purpose for life during their college years, but often they get the most help outside of the curriculum. Too many others go years beyond college before they muster enough honesty and humility to say their lives are empty.

Some false notion of intellectualism appears to be keeping many academic communities from addressing our most basic questions. Until the campus rediscovers this role of helping individuals search for and find meaning, we should not be surprised at the devastating consequences of spiritual and moral poverty in our society.

To my mind, this is currently our nation's greatest need, yet so many who should be taking the lead suffer from the tyranny of the urgent. We would rather talk about form than substance. Humanism has proved powerless to change human nature—the root cause of social decay. If Kristol is correct that humanism is the predominant religion in America today, then on the basis of its record, the universities should open it up for reexamination.

If this freedom existed on the campus, if students were encouraged to look honestly at their moral and spiritual underpinnings, and if society recognized more of its college graduates as persons of moral commitment and purpose, then society would recognize that our institutions of higher learning have an important purpose that society could support. Not only for the next few years, but as long as our society exists.

A Finer Order,
A More General Happiness

Stephen K. Bailey

Both essays about the future and essays about the past can be exercises in imagination, but only the former deals with malleable events. As Harlan Cleveland put it a few years back, "Futurists...analyze what might happen later to illuminate what should happen earlier." What might happen to American colleges and universities can, of course, be healthily disturbing to those charged with making something "happen earlier." If one were to choose the most disquieting academic trends currently observable, and extrapolate them for the next quarter century, the resulting scenario would be gloomy indeed. For example:

• Two thirds of all private colleges have disappeared. Their plants have been assigned a variety of welfare, health, or private-enterprise roles. A few campuses in rural areas are ghost towns— replete with shattered windows and cobwebs. Occasionally an abandoned dormitory is kept in reasonable external repair by intermittent bands of squatter youth.

• The undergraduate sections of our great private universities are finishing schools for the bored and cynical offspring of America's affluent. Not since eighteenth-century England have a nation's leading universities fallen into greater disrepute. Academic freedom has long since been compromised by ribaldry and petty insurrections. Professors have become entertainers or pedantic functionaries assigned to initialing the chits of meretricious status.

• Graduate schools of arts and sciences have dwindled in number and quality. Graduate student unions have improved the

154

emoluments of TAs, but the mustiness of intellectual pursuits has made "advanced" intellectual life dreary beyond measure. Serious intellectual work has settled elsewhere, especially in for-profit and not-for-profit research centers.

• Graduate professional training, because of its cost, has shifted to a handful of public institutions at the state and regional level.

• Half of the urban community colleges were destroyed by arson and pillage in the great center-city racial revolts of the mid-eighties; those that remain are half empty, for the economy still has no jobs for 40 percent of urban youths under 25.

• All but a dozen of America's land-grant universities and state colleges are dreary holding tanks for feckless suburban and small-city youth. The professoriat is totally unionized and tenured in by contract. The few academic administrators with spark look forward to the next decade when, after an interminable 35 years, an increasing number of wizened faculty will have retired and some new appointments can be made.

• Consumerism, a fad in the late seventies and early eighties, was defeated toward the end of the century by crowded court dockets and by the political power and protective stratagems of faculty.

• Women and minorities are still massively underrepresented in academic life. Disheartened and angered by decades of affirmative action subterfuge and reverse discrimination ploys, they have found more lucrative and exciting opportunities elsewhere.

• Nontraditional programs are ubiquitous. The society is pasted over with certificates. Employees and professional societies have long been giving their own examinations in order to reestablish by demonstrations of merit what was destroyed by eroding standards and runaway credentialing.

• Both public and private institutions of higher education are monitored and "line-itemed" by green-eyeshade types in state capitals and in Washington. Computers programmed for cost/benefit analyses on triangulated formulas of usable square footage, FTEs, and faculty/student ratios inform state allocations to public and private colleges and universities—and even to the tiny subdivisions thereof.

• Vocationalism has triumphed. On-the-job apprenticeships account for 70 percent of all postsecondary training. In consequence, the total social investment in higher education has dropped, in terms of 1975 definitions of GNP, by more than 50 percent. Culture is kitsch. Most people teleview their lives away.

This montage of nightmares has a degree of probability directly proportional to the number of shrugs of inevitability accompanying its reading. None of it is inexorable. All of it is possible. Avoidance of these possibilities will not occur by magic incantations. Salvation will come by increments of multiple devotions: the warnings of pamphleteers; tough and principled decisions by trustees and administrators; self-examinations as well as institutional examinations by faculty; courageous disciplinary action by state chartering agencies and accrediting bodies; responsible consumer pressures by students and parents; political virtuosity on the part of state and national educational associations; analytic rigor and self-denying ordinances by government auditors and program monitors; acts of statesmanship by key political leaders and their staffs; responsible reporting and comment by the media.

All of these energies can make a difference if they are motivated by a reaffirmation of the values served by the academy when it is most faithful to itself. If the worst of the present can be extrapolated into a dismal scenario, the best of it can be extrapolated into an equally compelling but far more felicitous one. For example:

• As a result of careful stock taking, curriculum modification, state tuition-equalization schemes, federal tax incentives, and an enormous influx of foreign students, private higher education has taken a new lease on life. Eighty percent of the private institutions extant in 1975 are still vigorous in 2000. Taken together with public higher education they represent a rich diversity of educational offerings, for individuals and groups of all ages.

• As a result of faculty development programs, the winnowing of some chaff, and the extraordinary quality of the limited number of new instructional hirings, undergraduate education has blossomed. A new core is addressed to the existential realities of longer lifespans and is purveyed through a variety of media and schedules to vast segments of the population of all ages.

• Graduate schools of arts and sciences are bursting with talent and excitement as America recognizes that the phrase "an overeducated society" is a contradiction in terms. The most intractable problems of mankind—peace, food, energy, health, biospheric viability, prejudice, poverty, urban sordidness, boredom—receive disciplinary focus, interdisciplinary creativity, and stable public funding.

• Professional training has become....

In short, optimistic counterparts to the doleful items noted previously can easily be conjectured. My bets are on "the sunnier side of doubt."

It is strange how strange a mood of possible optimism seems. The stridency of the sixties and the litigiousness and decrementalism of the seventies seem to have blocked out our capacity to hear positive and prophetic sounds. This is unfortunate. The only way to dispel society's massive case of the "blahs" is to posit some desirables, some friendly possibles, and then to work like hell for their approximation. Such desirables must, it seems to me, avoid romanticism. The following propositions must be understood and internalized:

• Equal educational opportunity cannot mean equal educational results, whatever the perceived injustices of the universe, but it can mean a far greater closing of the gap than we have achieved to date.
• The progressive lowering of standards is the well-endowed's ultimate patronizing of the socially disadvantaged.
• Higher education means higher effort which means short-term psychic pain; those who cannot be taught or otherwise induced to bear the pain of thought and the itchiness of concentration should not waste their money.
• Academic freedom is no less subject to scrupulous moral inquiry than any other freedom, but it must be protected at all costs against interruption and abnegation by fleeting passions.

How will we know if higher education is alive and well in the year 2000? The following bench marks suggest my own biases:

• Individuals, without regard to accidents of birth or fortune, have recurring opportunities for advanced study throughout their lives;
• people of all economic classes and social groups, and from many nations, have a reasonable possibility of choosing among a variety of types, sizes, and prestige levels of colleges and universities;
• combinations of low tuition in public institutions, strengthened government support to increase choice among public and private institutions, limited lifelong learning entitlements, a new influx of students from abroad, and facilitated savings and loan-repayment arrangements tied to long-term tax withholdings for parents and students have given the first two propositions an effective reality base;
• a full-employment economy and total portability of fringe benefits have reduced job insecurity and increased the lateral mobility of faculty;

• bargaining contracts, intermittent hard times, and a responsible consumerism have given a new tone and commitment to the faculty work ethic;

• income differentials between college-educated and noncollege-educated have become so insignificant as to make people choose higher education for its contributions to the quality of existence rather than to probable lifetime earnings;

• curricula are highly varied, but each student's pursuit shows evidence of careful design; standards of graduation are tougher than ever at all postsecondary levels.

The ultimate test of the quality of our higher education, of course, will be the condition of our civilization. If an increasing number of our citizens have come to understand that we live in a natural world whose laws we twist or violate at our peril; that the dehumanizing aspects of urbanization and technology must be continuously fought; that there are no "zero-sum" games in the world of human values, only trade-offs and optimizations; that privacy and community are necessary complements; that massive income disparities ultimately threaten the rich as much as the poor; that nations as well as individuals need superegos; that humanistic creations and appreciations are mankind's great shields against boredom; that prejudice and discrimination are subhuman abominations; that because two people think differently, neither need be wicked; that never-ending discovery is the most glorious manifestation of the human condition; if they have come to understand all of this, then higher education will have proved its worth and vitality.

Nearly 80 years ago, in an obscure novel, H. G. Wells made the essential point. "If humanity," he wrote, "cannot develop an education far beyond anything that is now provided, if it cannot collectively invent devices and solve problems on a much richer, broader scale than it does at the present time, it cannot hope to achieve any very much finer order or any more general happiness than it now enjoys."

Who Runs the Show?

George W. Bonham

There are certain milestones in the passing of time—the ends of
decades, centuries, millennia—when we are tempted to stand
back and measure our progress since the last marker, and to gauge
our progress toward the next. I'm given to such temptations as
much as anyone, particularly when academics talk about that
favorite if rather arcane word "governance." When serious people
are asked these days who is in charge of the universities, the
answer is usually, "No one." Or the question occasions a series of
guffaws, which, though avoiding the issue, suggests the delicacy
of the question.

Nonetheless, at the peril of oversimplification, I believe that a
certain *fin-de-siècle* occurrence has in fact taken place so far as the
organizational functioning and structure of many academic institutions are concerned. Myths such as faculty autonomy and academic freedom are important enough to sustain, since they bear
operational values of their own. But they are myths nonetheless.

In the first century of this nation's life, our colleges were in the
main the creation of individual leaders, clerics in part; and such
colleges perished or flourished according to the particular talents
and fortunes of these eighteenth- and nineteenth-century college
presidents. Times were usually hard, but there is a certain nostal-
gic charm in historical accounts of those early, fragile colleges.
Such histories were almost invariably idiosyncratic, reflecting the
personalities of particular individuals usually given to selfless service and faith in their particular sense of destiny.

The late nineteenth century, of course, saw the development of modern industrial society. This evolution, together with the emergence of vastly more ambitious public colleges and universities resulting from the Morrill Act, produced academic institutions much more akin to their present counterparts. The period continued to give rise to some extraordinary academic leaders and empire builders, but academic matters were increasingly organized along vastly more complex lines more or less parliamentary in structure, but also suggesting in part the organizational character of corporate and governmental organizations. Two dominant factors favorable to such consensual structures made twentieth-century academic institutions work, often well: The first was the prevailing broad sense of purpose within the academic community and without; the second, that American society was capable of and willing to support an ever-growing higher education enterprise committed to universal access to education beyond the high school. Almost coincidental to the celebration of the nation's bicentennial, however, neither assumption is any longer being shared by the majority of people who make decisions. There are many reasons for this turn of events. Ideologically, the earlier campus battles over Vietnam and civil rights left their particular heritage. It is difficult to argue that such battles did not in the end benefit the country, but the politicization of the campuses also left its mark on salient questions such as, Who represented the university?

The crisis of authority that has overtaken many, though by no means all, institutions of learning is perhaps not all that different from that which has affected other major social institutions. But higher education has far fewer resources to resolve this crisis than have more hierarchical organizations. The fact is that the academic machinery has seriously broken down. Things have simply become unhinged. They no longer work very well, though the appearance of a working structure is generally maintained. Initiative and creativity are largely gone, for the initiatives and creativity of one group on campus represent a threat to the cherished turf of another. It is not a balance of terror, to be sure, but a balance of symbolic posturing, of shadowboxing over issues not substantive but procedural. In a period of often dramatically declining resources, the question is no longer what is best for the larger whole but how do I keep my own boat from rocking more than necessary. What one frequently sails along on are scraps of status reinforcement rather than issues on which prudent decisions can be made. Michael D. Cohen and James G. Marsh, in their book *Leadership and Ambiguity*, speak to this idea of status function in an interesting way: "For many people, the process and structure of university governance are more important than the outcome—

at least within wide ranges of possible outcomes. Participation is not a means but an end. Academic institutions easily become *process-* rather than *output*-oriented. Goals provide scant evidence of whether the output of the decision process within academe is desirable, but participation in the process is a conspicuous certification of status. Individuals establish themselves as important by virtue of their rights of participation in the governance of the institution."

This imposition of symbolic power certification over issues of real substance strikes me, I'll confess, as particularly tragic in a field where truth and the force of ideas were once the dominant enticements that attracted men and women in the first place. It is a tragedy that among some of the most talented and intellectually gifted groups in our society, principles of balanced judgment and merit are now so widely subjected to narrow issues of academic sovereignty. One need not spell out the extent of the resultant pettiness that seems to have affected so many academic institutions.

Though we can hardly rejoice over such increasing concern with academic minutiae, these are surely lessons for those who look at the prospects for academic vitality in the third century. The academic penchant to fight over a barren no-man's-land is not alone a matter of certifying and recertifying status; it is also due to the growing dominance of educational institutions by a gray middle-management bureaucracy. Some academic observers see the rise of this "bureauversity" as a necessary response to governmental demands for accountability. The complexity of modern institutions themselves, however, makes such layers of bureaucratic management inevitable. But though such academic bureaucracies arose out of certain managerial imperatives, they can by no means be regarded as machinery for brilliant initiatives. Bureaucracies exist in part for themselves. They have a life of their own, and their relationship with the higher calling of the campuses they serve may be more accidental than intentional. Managerial processes and events now seem to have a way of escaping the grasp and control of even the most competent academic managers. Warren Bennis, president of the University of Cincinnati and a leading authority on modern management, recites this event at his own institution as a poignant illustration of how matters can get off the track:

> On the first real day of spring, two beautiful trees in the infancy of bloom are chopped down to make room for cars to turn down a campus driveway. Everybody is outraged. Students pack into

my office to tell me about it. A few are hysterical and crying. I leave my office and walk over to the little grass plot—there is so little green on our campus—to see a man with a small hand power saw, cleaning and stacking up the milk white wood into neat piles.

A crowd of some 200 students and faculty stand around and hiss me as I break through the circle to speak to him. "Man, am I glad you're here. They're ready to crucify me." It turns out he is not employed by the university. He works for a local contractor. I could never find out who was responsible: the landscape artist who designed the new plot with poodle hedges, or his boss, the landscape architect; the director of planning, or his boss, the head of the physical plant; the vice president for management and finance, the university building committee, the executive vice president the committee reports to....

When I called them all together they numbered 20, and they were innocents all. All of us. Bureaucracies are beautiful mechanisms for the evasion of responsibility and guilt.

The events described here are, of course, not confined to academic institutions but are part and parcel of large organizations everywhere. It would be idyllic and romantic to imagine that E. F. Schumacher's notions of "small is beautiful" are any more applicable to complex academic institutions than to macro-organizations elsewhere. The innumerable converts he has made among American academics are more likely enchanted by his theories than by the possibilities for practical applications to their own circumstances. Only avowed poverty and dire conditions will bring academic people to a willingness to consider alternatives to the standard nondecision-making process.

Shimer College, an innovative college with a past generic connection to the University of Chicago, is now considering a decentralized collective self-governance structure as one alternative for the next century. "Cooperative administration," says a Shimer planning document, "for private institutions of higher education is the forgotten alternative. The concept of cooperative self-governance for a college or university is as old as the twelfth-century 'community of scholars.'" However, the purity of the original notion seems to have become extinct during the intervening centuries. Recently, cooperative worker management has been revived as a promising antidote to the human problems in industry. Cooperative self-governance, with suitable modern adjustments, deserves another try in academia.

Usually, instincts toward Spartan collectives of the learned and their student acolytes issue from the creative wellsprings of academic utopians or arise from the threat of bankruptcy. But even the smallest learning communities, alas, must now deal with extra-educational issues. These range from a knowledge of the tax laws to the effective recruitment of tuition-paying students to keep body and soul together. Corporate existence, no matter how modest, is no longer possible under present circumstances without providing for certain managerial talents and energies. Bureaucracies foster counterbureaucracies, and academic institutions in the next century are not likely to be any less burdened by such institutional baggage than now.

With the whole academic machinery increasingly creaking from old age, what corrections and fresh approaches might be found to make third-century colleges deal more effectively with third-century questions? Perhaps the slow and patient fine tuning of academic organizations is all one can hope and strive for. Fine tuning works well in our most established elite universities, but it is a model that must be increasingly questioned in 95 percent of all remaining institutions. For the fact must be stated that we are dealing here not with institutional weaknesses but increasingly with institutional paralysis. This spreading paralysis is perhaps more apparent to an outside observer than to campus inhabitants. Institutional circumstances may degenerate so gradually that what is diagnosed as paralysis by a visitor may be seen merely as a gradual adjustment to new circumstances by the players on the field.

But that there is paralysis is no longer in question. Adam Yarmolinsky, writing in *Daedalus*, says that institutional paralysis of higher education "is a result of four fundamental disjunctions within the university's body politic: the disjunction between faculty and administration; the disjunction between substantive planning and budgetary decision making; the disjunction between departmental structures and functional areas of university concern; and the disjunction between the theory of direct democracy and its practice in the university.

"No institution in the United States," continues Yarmolinsky, "puts more constraints on its administration than a university. The administration cannot hire or fire a faculty member on its own initiative. It cannot initiate a new course offering or modify or abandon an old one. It cannot determine the requirements for completion of a course of study or decide whether or not a student has met those requirements. And, in most cases, it can neither admit nor dismiss a student."

I share Yarmolinsky's view that academic administrations are perhaps the only modern form of management that is not legitimated as a substantive decision-making agency. Allowing for the moment that such a state of affairs did not hinder growth and creativity of our universities in the fifties and sixties, will the next few decades be so tolerant?

My answer is that they will not. Third-century institutions of learning must be participatory organizations, while guaranteeing against institutional paralysis; they must be durable and humane structures and yet allow for the needed initiatives and risk taking without which institutional survival seems ever less likely. They must attract leaders of extraordinary talents who will not be consumed by the day-to-day infighting over trivia and pork barreling. I know of no other managerial responsibility that is more likely to lead to defeat or at least to a Mexican standoff than what the typical academic president is now exposed to. He or she must deal not only with faculty, students, trustees, and alumni, but also with state coordinating boards, minorities and ethnics, the courts, funding agencies, local, state, and federal governments, town and gown, and sundry other agents of society, many of which presume that the president's motives, by definition, must somehow be misdirected. It is a wonder that men and women of talent and wisdom still vie for posts of academic presidencies when the likelihood of success has been reduced to that of a parliamentarian duck shoot. Academic presidents have become largely academic caretakers, and the long-term consequences of this diminution in leadership are not too difficult to anticipate.

No one can predict the future of academic institutions with any sense of accuracy. My own inclinations rest more on changes devoutly to be hoped for than on those that will actually take place. My first assumption rests on the likelihood that someone, somewhere, will finally discover that present academic governance works less and less well, and that something must be done about it.

I begin with the academic presidency. Since there is no corporate collectivity legally and in fact in charge, I would strengthen the office of the presidency while building in certain constitutional restraints on behalf of those affected by presidential decisions. An important assurance for leadership must be a provision for talent, and sufficient time to put that talent to work. Present selection procedures for presidents are elaborate and tedious. I have seen committees labor for a year or more before deciding on the appropriate candidate, only to discover a year later that it was all a grievous mistake. I don't know what the ideal method of selection should be, but I would argue that the care with which the selection process usually proceeds should be followed by a period of presid-

164

ing that extends beyond the traditional honeymoon period. Academic presidents are given rope, to be sure, but often not enough for them even to have the opportunity of hanging themselves. My own preference would be to write presidential contracts for five years, renewable for periods of three years thereafter. Evaluation of the president might proceed in tandem with his or her administration, but I would make certain that presidential dismissals could only occur under the most blatant circumstances of malfeasance or ineffectiveness. Academic boards now routinely fire their presidents on a majority vote, frequently swing votes that can change with the temperature in the boardroom. Often these turn out to be quixotic decisions to be regretted later on. Presidential dismissals should require a three fourths majority vote, and I would have the decisions on second and third contract renewals on a two thirds or three fourths majority vote.

One can argue that the last year of a president's tenure would carry all the frailties of a lame duck administration. But if presidential performance has in fact achieved certain widely shared goals, prospects are rather for a continuing term instead of nonrenewal. I would further encourage presidential risk taking by guaranteeing any academic president a tenured professorship at three fourths of the presidential salary. I have never found persuasive the argument that ex-presidents ought to leave their campuses after their service is complete. Quite the contrary: They are often more capable of insight once administrative burdens have been lifted from their shoulders.

I would make consonant changes in collegiate boards of trustees. One of the many academic myths is that academic boards are a godsend to mankind. They are in some cases, but in many others they are not. Where academic boards function effectively as whole committees, they can do praiseworthy work. But a growing number of boards are so politicized that it is difficult to know who speaks for whom. Public college and university boards appointed serially by governors of opposing parties can be inventions of the devil. While such matters are rarely talked about in polite company, it needs to be stated that any institutional leadership under such circumstances can be an exercise in futility.

So as to depoliticize public boards of universities, I would seek bipartisan appointments reflecting the political parties' strength in the state legislature. Board terms of office should be constitutionally limited to six years, with one third going off each year. In addition to the gubernatorially selected (and in some cases publicly elected) trustees, I would include a minority of campus constituencies of administrators, faculty, and students, perhaps adding 30 percent to the board's total composition. Here I would follow the lead of the University of Massachusetts. Faculty and student initiatives are transmitted to the trustees by the administration. If not acted upon unfavorably within a given period of time, they automatically take effect.

For both public and private institutions, the role of faculty needs to be clarified. Faculty unionization will continue, and I see this not as a particular threat to either teacher or administrator. If anything, it will help resolve the issues of who is to decide what. Faculty senates have on the whole become useless appendages, and they will be relied on less and less. Faculty must retain their traditional responsibility for teaching content and scholarship. But administrators are the ones who determine what kind of education is necessary for what kind of student, and what parts of their campus operations must be curtailed, enlarged, or held the same. It is inevitable and essential that the area where these decisions intersect must be split into mutually recognized spheres of competence. The faculty may be the last to know of the flight of students from their departments. Questions of survival are increasingly *institutional* questions, and it is not possible for individual faculty or departments to make such allocation decisions without full integration with the whole.

To the extent that one can identify wise and prudent individuals, I think it highly useful to have faculty and student representation on the board. There are cogent arguments against both kinds of representation, of course, but if the parliamentary approach to decision making is to work at all, I would rather have matters resolved at the level that counts, which is the legally constituted board of trustees. With a strong and semitenured president in charge, special pleadings from important constituencies become not impediments but rather reflections to the campus of the ongoing debate over the course and direction of the institution.

No single strategy is adaptable to 3,000 colleges and universities. They vary enormously in their histories, traditions, and outlooks. But third-century academic institutions must provide for themselves constitutionally built-in guarantees of continuity, moving from their present ad hoc nature to collaborative groups of strong-willed and dedicated professionals that have some chance at survival and integrity in an increasingly chaotic world.

V
The Third Century

A Confederacy of Concerns

Allan W. Ostar

"The world, in sum, does not proceed like an Aristotelian syllogism," wrote Charles Weingarter. "The damnedest things keep happening." A case in point: At the beginning of this decade it was assumed by administrators and policy makers that the enrollment growth of the fifties and sixties would continue through the seventies as greater percentages of high school graduates enrolled in college. The reverse has happened. The percentage of high school graduates attending college has decreased from a high of 55 percent in 1968 to 47 percent in 1973. The decline has occurred across the board: men, women, minorities.

The wrench thrown into this progression of growing enrollments was money: Price is a major factor in determining college attendance. Under circumstances of rising student charges, demand for education becomes elastic. A second unforeseen factor straining the ability of families to pay for college is "sibling interval." Demographers at the University of Michigan Population Studies Center have found that while families formed in the 1930s averaged just over two births at four-year intervals, those families formed in the fifties and sixties averaged over three births per family at intervals just under two years. Beginning in 1969, the average American family would have to support more than one student in college during a four-year period. Additionally, the effects of inflation and the job market have had a major but difficult to measure impact on college enrollments.

We must also consider that men and women, not an unseen hand, guide the direction of history. Things happen only because human beings cause them to happen. If we want something to happen—if we want to eradicate poverty, if we want to give everyone two free years of college—we can. But we can't do everything we want (and, of course, not everyone wants the same thing) and so it becomes a matter of weighted interests, priorities, indecision. With powerful advocates on all sides of every issue, it is difficult to determine just what Americans want.

With these qualifiers tucked away like insurance policies, I would like to begin by reviewing the trend mentioned above—the elastic demand for education apparently created because tuition costs have risen faster than the consumer price index and the wholesale price index, particularly in public institutions.

In declaring his candidacy for the 1976 Democratic Presidential nomination, Congressman Morris K. Udall identified the issues of the campaign as the three E's: the economy, energy, and the environment. Actually, Udall probably identified the ruling concerns of our public and private lives for the remaining 25 years of this century at least. The resolution of these issues depends upon another E: education. I believe it is the most important of the four. Education is the problem-solving tool. It will provide the researchers, the manpower, the technicians, and the informed public that together form the basis of the decision-making process. The quality of life in the year 2000 will depend upon the support given to higher education. We thus cannot afford to have it viewed as a commodity with an elastic demand.

The system of financing in the year 2000 must guarantee access. I do not envision a system radically different from the state financing pattern now employed. A national system operated by the federal government would not improve upon the efficient operation of the present funding system; if anything it would add another layer of bureaucracy. The authorization and appropriation processes would become even more cumbersome. However, I do think the federal government can encourage states to maintain funding levels adequate for the support of quality education and encouraging access. If constructed properly, federal student aid programs can be used to dissuade states from raising tuitions. A federal institutional aid program based on some cost-of-education formula would also help colleges and universities in their efforts to hold down tuition. I hope that long before the millennium these programs and policies will be in effect, halting the shift of more and more of the cost of education to the students and their families.

The financial approach must go beyond guaranteed access for the high school graduate age group. Even in 1975 we found that opportunities for self-renewal and reeducation were becoming increasingly important: for the housewife with grown children who seeks a new career; for the worker who seeks job advancement; for the technician whose field is changing; for the retiree with an active mind and time to spare.

Over the next 25 years, the need for such opportunities will increase greatly, for reasons that have been enumerated so many times they need only be mentioned briefly. The pace of change in our society is incredible—scientific knowledge doubles every 10 years. Automation is being applied to all aspects of our lives, from the assembly line to food service. More work is accomplished in less time resulting in more leisure time. It has been estimated that within 40 years almost all human activity now regarded as work will have been assumed by technological devices. If true, then by the year 2000 we will be approximately halfway into the automated age, with a decrease in the number of blue-collar and skilled workers and an increase in the number of white-collar and professional workers.

What kinds of new work will they be engaged in? Management consultant Peter Drucker and the futurist Alvin Toffler have both predicted that the currency of the future economy will be knowledge. Drucker has noted that in the late 1970s the "knowledge industries" will account for one half of the Gross National Product. By the year 2000, two thirds, or perhaps even three quarters, of the GNP will be generated by these enterprises. Toffler also believes that the "challenges facing the modern enterprise are knowledge-gathering, truth-requiring dilemmas." We are becoming a society in which the generation, dissemination, and organization of knowledge will be the primary occupations of a great many people in various fields.

Chief among the knowledge and information enterprises are colleges and universities. They are the basic information enterprise and their continuing dilemma has been to preserve an objective climate in which knowledge and truth can be pursued. With the coming emphasis upon knowledge as a primary factor in production and commerce, education and work will become more and more synonymous. The distinction between the world of education and the world of work will disappear as individuals move between the knowledge center of the university and the information functions of their work. Learning will become an integral part of the daily work as technicians, administrators, and management consultants apply knowledge to new problems.

Colleges and universities will assume new positions of importance in the world of work by providing more opportunities for ad hoc learning. IBM may be able to operate training classes in programming computers. But the job of knowing which facts to select in order to program a computer must still be learned in a college or university.

The temporary or ad hoc students for whom we must provide represent only an extension of current patterns of part-time learning. According to the Office of Education, 20 percent of the total college population in 1970 was part-time; by 1974 their numbers had grown to 37.1 percent of the total. Between 1972 and 1974 the full-time population grew by 5.8 percent while the part-time population grew by 39.2 percent.

The number of part-time learners will increase as more learning opportunities are opened up through time-free, space-free options. These would include classes in the evening, on weekends, or in concentrated time periods coinciding with work breaks. Place options will also increase: Learning will be offered on the campus, in places of business, in community centers, and in the home. None of these are new concepts. But in the next 25 years they must cease being novelties and become part of the accepted learning scheme.

What a student may learn in a university in the year 2000 provides fascinating speculation, especially given our society's tendency to revise history. It is certain that more technical matter will be taught, probably in fields of knowledge yet unknown. I do not foresee, however, nor do I hope to see, a proliferation of specialist majors added to the departmental structure we now have.

As specialists have developed the art of our technologies to a high degree, the result has been a growing complex of problems that involve not one technical aspect but many. While the temptation may be great to prepare even more superspecialists, what we need today and will continue to need are interspecialists: individuals with interdisciplinary backgrounds who can look at problems in terms of the interrelationships involved and arrive at compatible solutions. Any resolution of a local energy dilemma must be related to the environment, the economy of the area, and the lifestyle of the community. We cannot look solely to the nuclear physicist to build a power plant.

To accomplish this, the current departmental organization of our colleges and universities must be restructured. By the year 2000 I suspect we will no longer have departments of chemistry, biology, physics, and geology, but will have instead a physical sciences learning center. Instead of departments of mathematics, engineering, industrial design, and cybernetics, a technology learning center; a center of human services instead of departments of sociology, psychology, and criminology. Faculty will become learning resources instead of simply lecturers. The teaching process will reflect the fact that not every student learns at the same rate or begins at the same level. The emphasis will be on personalized learning programs, just as it is now on lecture learning.

We now have the technology for individualized learning—cassettes, videotapes, computers. By the turn of the century, we should have perfected the art of learning technology in order to apply it to maximum individual gain. Faculty should be able to assume more comprehensive support roles as learning facilitators, mentors, and counselors.

Increasing technology and automation will not, should not, bring a decline in the liberal arts. Rather it ought to increase the need for liberal arts. Arnold Toynbee held that "the price of specialization is a myopic and distorted view of the universe. An effective specialist makes, all too often, a defective citizen and an inadequate specialist makes, all too often, a defective citizen and an inadequate human being." Toynbee's judgment is harsh, but he has a point: The more automated our technological society becomes, the greater will be our need for personal autonomy, for a sense of humanity, for a clear perception of the relationships between man and society. We will have an increasing need for a sound foundation in what I would like to call the cultural arts—a more appropriate designation than liberal arts.

Culture is that total environment in which we live and work. Culture is the result of those historical, economic, artistic, and social forces that operate on our lives; it is the pressure to which we respond—consciously or unconsciously—in shaping our own history. We cannot build the culture of the twenty-first century unless we understand the cultural forces of the past and present. If colleges and universities do not strengthen the cultural arts and integrate them into the learning process, we will run the risk of producing "defective human beings."

Additionally, the curriculum must expand the sense of humanity to include the perception of our students as citizens of the world. We must develop study programs that instill a sense of world community and of shared interests among cultures. Lecturer and former ambassador Edwin O. Reischauer has noted that "worldwide capacities for disruption and destruction are growing much faster than the economic well-being of the less-developed countries." We have to recognize not only our own expectations for the future, but also those of others. We have to realize that a new discipline in our lives is necessary if we are to free our fellow world citizens from poverty and hunger.

The internationalism of the curriculum should not be directed toward preparing experts in international studies. It should enable every businessman, every student, every tourist, every touring artist, to be sensitive to and to respect the cultural differences represented around the world. The curriculum must provide an international influence for people who will never leave the country, who, when they read of an oil increase or a famine, will respond with some understanding of the human needs involved.

The responsibilities of higher education will be far greater than they are now. Our colleges and universities will serve broader and more diverse segments of the population, contribute to the resolution of domestic problems, play a vital role in the health of our economy, and lend their expertise in overcoming the barriers to world peace.

These increased responsibilities will entail changes, certainly more than the structural and programmatic ones discussed here. Beyond these procedural changes there is a philosophical issue: What is the ultimate purpose of a college education? We have a system of higher education geared to the individual goals and aspirations appropriate to a competitive society. In a capitalistic democracy that honors free enterprise, private property, and individualism, it is assumed that individual goals are compatible with those of society. Higher education that benefits the individual benefits the society. This is in large part the justification for public investment in education.

However, a question is beginning to surface and it will command more attention as we approach the twenty-first century: Do students recognize a higher purpose beyond self-improvement and advancement? Do they recognize that the quality of their own lives depends upon what they contribute to the quality of life for everyone?

This question was heightened for me by a trip to the People's Republic of China. The educational system of the People's Republic rejects education for personal gain or fame. Its educational philosophy is the reverse of our own: By serving the needs of the larger society, individuals will benefit.

One cannot help but relate the gains the People's Republic has made to this educational philosophy; it prods one to consider the problems we confront in this country and the new sense of community and discipline that will be necessary to solve them. Those problems will not be resolved if each individual seeks to achieve personal success with no thought to the larger issues that are involved.

Higher education is responsible for stressing values, for acculturating lifestyles, and for helping to identify goals. The ultimate question for higher education is whether it can be creative enough to maintain individual freedom while at the same time developing an educational value system that puts service to society above service to self.

Beyond the Cloister

Morris T. Keeton

I foresee three developments occurring during the next quarter century: a continuing increase in the degree of diversification and individualization of postsecondary educational services; a growing sophistication in the assessment of what people have learned or achieved; and a growing specification and differentiation of standards. These are intertwined and needed developments that will nevertheless be strongly resisted, and all present difficult tasks conceptually, administratively, and politically. Yet I think that however blunderingly we go about helping or hindering their realization, powerful social forces will press in the direction of these changes. Barring some cataclysm, we will evolve in these directions.

The postsecondary learning of the future will and should differ markedly from that of today. In content, in the ways it is made accessible, in the ways it is combined with other activities and interests, in the balance between classroom learning and other arenas, and in the meanings that its new content will bring—in all of these ways it will differ from learning today. Not that radical discontinuities are to be expected: The signs of these changes are already in our data.

In the social sciences and in the humanities especially there should be, within the next quarter century, not only continuing accumulation of data, but emerging intellectual syntheses. These new organizing concepts will begin to do for the study of society and of human concerns, though perhaps on a less grand scale, what such syntheses as those of Newton and Einstein did for the physical sciences. We should thus have not just more knowledge, but transformed views of the world. In this sense, the meaning of what we have learned will have changed.

Implied is the expectation that what we are learning today will need to be unlearned tomorrow. Those of us who still will not have reached 100 years of age by the year 2000 should be preparing to continue updating ourselves if we wish to enjoy and to understand the life of which we will be a part.

It was once thought that the best years of life for learning were over by the time a person had reached intermediate school. This idea sprang from a conception of learning as essentially the assimilation of information, not as the transformation of experience into ever more maturing insights, or as transformation of the self into an ever more responsive, responsible, and effective participant in a society also in need of transformation. Now it is becoming clear that in personality development, in the maturing of conceptual capabilities, and in moral development, the years ripest for these transformative stages arrive in most people after the time (so-called "college age") that our culture has allocated for formal education. Now that the late and complex maturing of persons is becoming clearer, we must rethink the old limitations as to when, with whom, and about what the processes of genuinely higher education should unfold.

To be well educated in this new world will not admit of treating one's ongoing learning as a matter principally for sabbaticals. In tomorrow's world we shall have devised a new structuring of the relationships among work, study, and leisure. Perhaps these concepts themselves will be among those transformed by the added knowledge in its new conceptual packagings. If by 1980 the right of older adults to have their "twelfth year" of governmentally assisted learning has been established for those who missed it in their teens, then by 2000 this right will surely have moved on to the equivalent of a fourteenth or a sixteenth year, though I would hope that by then the labeling of education achieved by year levels will have lost most of whatever force and meaning it still retains.

In any event, access to learning in the near future should reflect improvements with respect to both financing and delivery. With financing, we shall probably never settle on an ideal percentage of the Gross National Product to go into education. It seems more likely that we will have to recognize a limit of tax-supported expenditure for direct support of education beyond which there sets in a law of diminishing social returns. Already the needs of health, transportation, environmental protection, and the administration of justice begin to compete significantly with those of education.

We can hope, and should insist, that nationalistically oriented defense expenditure gives way increasingly to an outlay that is directed more toward world security and to its being a lower proportion of the national budget than it is now. Nevertheless, the mix of investment should continue to engage our best thinking and our active debate. From this mélée there will probably emerge a continuing enlargement of sums spent on postsecondary education. But we will be, and should be, hard pressed to get the best yield, since the demand for money will far exceed the funds available. The most radical improvements in financing that I can envisage will not be sheer add-ons to direct support of education. Instead there will be gains achieved by new trade-offs in which a dollar spent for facilities or personnel for one social purpose (health, environmental protection, and so on) will be planned to serve another purpose at the same time.

It is on the basis of this last idea that I foresee the possibility of a diversification of the systems of control over learning optunities and delivery of learning services. I do not know whether such alternatives, with their difficult ethical and administrative problems, could reverse the trend toward exclusive control over higher education by publicly controlled institutions. What has happened to secondary education as privately controlled schools have been driven out of business is, in terms of universal access, admirable, but in terms of quality and variety, lamentable. It appears that a similar fate is in store for higher education if no better alternative is devised. Given the costs of higher education, the level of current taxation, the state of the economy, and the effects of all of these matters upon disposable income, our lip service to privately controlled and operated colleges and universities is probably doomed to be just lip service. Surely the rising size of state and federal education bureaucracies and budgets, the increasing controls ranging from so-called coordination to outright regulation, and the increasing demands of institutions for higher proportions of governmental support are not going to wither merely because people blanch before the perils of state and federal control.

Whatever resolutions are adopted for the financing and control of higher education, the magnitude of national effort and investment put into it will continue to grow. Why? Because with every move to make technology more sophisticated, to cope with more rapid communication and transportation, to manage a more interdependent world, to deal with more intricate intercultural relationships—with every such effort the need for education to reflect upon purpose and direction, as well as to help with instrumenta-

178

tion, becomes greater. Moreover, the recent upsurge of enrollments of older students is no mere fad tied to momentary needs for employment or status. It relates as well to a breakaway from assumptions that confined the scope and depth of education and restricted it largely to prevocational periods of life. In addition, some changes are occurring in the liberation of individuals from earlier restrictions upon their opportunities and their rights, especially in the continuing attacks upon ethnic biases, sex biases, and other discriminatory social patterns. These changes will make for changes of climate, content, and participation in higher education.

In a recent essay prepared for the Cooperative Assessment of Experiential Learning, Cyril O. Houle of the University of Chicago has traced three periods in the uses made of experiential learning by the governing institutions of Western society. There was a trend, following the medieval period, "to move outward from cloistered instruction in basic texts toward direct firsthand experience." Then, in the nineteenth century, an effort in the reverse direction took place and is still in effect. As a consequence, academia has on the whole been too radically separated in its work from the experiential inputs essential to the best instruction. As James Coleman's research and analysis suggest, there is no one ideal mix of abstraction and experience for every learning need. There are, instead, many ways to create a mix that badly misses even a reasonable approximation to the ideal; we have generally returned too much to the cloister, in mind if not in physical location. Therefore, Houle is quite correct in saying not only that we may "have to invent as many new structures, concepts, and processes as did our forefathers in the last hundred years," but also that "above all, we must cultivate a new spirit that accepts the educative value and worth of all experience, not merely that which is devoted to scholarly study or which is guided at every step by professors."

Diversification in postsecondary education will result from the interplay of a number of the trends just cited: New knowledge and knowledge systems call for more, more complex, and more varied curricular offerings, with more room for lag in some parts of higher education than in others. New clienteles bring both new pedagogical needs and new logistical problems. The new learning possibilities dictated by developing understanding of the maturing of human beings will open up both new content and new timetables and strategies for learning. The ongoing effort to attack the next targets of discrimination (in access, institutional practices, and curricular content) will continue to produce locally divergent responses, and both diverse legislative enactments and diversely applied litigaton will reinforce these trends.

With all of this diversification will go still further individualization of services. Deep American commitments to the primacy of the individual will continue and will underlie this trend. Computer technology assists us in combining mass delivery of some elements of service with individual options as to their combination, sequence, and pattern. Our leisure and affluence and the combination of public support for education with private opportunity to pay for different or more services will further this effect. Since the individual's role in choosing educational goals and learning methods has a recognizable effect upon the depth and efficiency of learning, pedagogical influences will also add pressure to the trend toward individualization.

As diversification and individualization grow, our present method of reporting what has been learned and how well it has been learned will become increasingly inadequate to the need for clear and truthful communication of the outcomes of postsecondary education. Consumer demands will call for improvement in ascertaining the results and reporting them correctly. Also the other users of the "product" of higher education—employers, for example—will want better information.

The great obstacles to supplying better information will be the lack of know-how among assessors and the failure of will to do the job. External political and economic pressures will have to supplement whatever idealism can be mustered among educators to induce them to develop something better than the present system of grades, credits, and degrees with their minimally valid and reliable information as to achievement and competence.

More difficult and more important even than these changes in assessing and reporting what students have learned and achieved will be the struggle with standards. The standards of a society, including its educational standards, are enormously resistant to change. In a sense they are the key to a society's weaknesses and to its viability, to its worth in human fulfillment. Since they express what is viewed as most worthwhile in practice, they are the most vehemently defended element of the social fabric when attacked. Also as technological and ideological changes occur, standards are the most important thing about a society to change if its potential is to be realized. Because of the difficulty of head-on attack upon standards (objectors are heretics and radicals in the common perception), they are often undermined and observed in the breach well before their inadequacy can be openly acknowledged and deliberately reconsidered.

In the United States today we have both great confusion about educational standards and a major need for clarification and diversification of standards. Much of what passes for good practice and high standards is class-biased, ethnically biased, sex-biased, colored by biases of professionalism in both the disciplines and the professions, poorly coordinated with employers' needs, and anachronistic in light of our knowledge of pedagogy and human development needs. The effort to clarify and improve standards is complicated by the competition among forces seeking to control postsecondary education, each with its own axes to grind over what is permissible or ought to be encouraged. These competitors and controllers include state regulatory authorities, regional accrediting bodies, specialized accrediting agencies, federal watchdogs concerned with everything from consumer protection to affirmative action to due process, as well as lobbyists for good causes and institutions of higher education seeking to preserve their autonomy.

The idea that some clear and adequate system can emerge to proclaim to all just what is best and most important strikes me as utopian in the extreme. The best that we can hope for—and perhaps the best also in terms of long-range value—is a growing acceptance of the fact that a society such as that of the year 2000 will require people with a great variety of distinctive achievements; that it will need ways both for people to gain these different results efficiently and to have the credentials attesting to them respected. With such a climate of acceptance for diverse credentials there may also develop a growing array of institutions in which standards of achievement and good practice for different purposes are enforced and expressed by means of diverse credentials attesting with greater accuracy than today to what their holders have done and can do.

For those who want higher education to make a difference in the quality of life in the future, this difficult struggle over new learning options and new standards may be one of the most productive in the next quarter century.

Notes From a Diary

James A. Norton

N otes from a diary: September 2000.

No one with a concern for his reputation would have dared predict in 1975 the outcome of the struggles for governance of universities that were to come in the next quarter century. There had been enough experiences in the preceding decade when a one-week prediction could be hazardous, even fatal, to the careers of some persons. As the nation's bicentennial approached, the contending, conflicting, confusing turmoil of society seemed to have caught higher education in its whirl, and no one was sure whether the enterprise was being carried to destruction or Oz.

The issues around which the struggles took place were real and deep. Basic among them was the right of a person who was to be served to have a say about the type and quality of service. This was an outgrowth, in a way, of the civil rights movement and its demands for self-determination; it was the precursor of a horizontal society. Another issue that came from the civil rights movement was the affirmative action program. Collective bargaining struggles were a leitmotiv of the period, as was the question of control over the stamp of approval, the credential.

Behind these issues of governance lay a fundamental confusion as to what the enterprise of higher education was all about. The Carnegie Commission on Higher Education at that time had just completed a lengthy research and policy study and testified that the first task for higher education was a "clarification of purposes." The struggle over governance was in some respects a substitution of process for undeveloped consensus, a searching rather than a movement toward established goals.

Sometimes during those years it seemed that the critical, rational examination of society higher education had long promoted may really have been too successful, especially when those in the communications industries began teaching everyone to demand rationality and justice faster than society could produce either. The myths that had held institutions together and justified purposes and processes proved inadequate for society generally and higher education particularly.

One issue around which fights occurred was called consumer protection. It is difficult to understand with our perspective of 25 years why it is that, in the memories of many people, the predominant attitude toward the consumer-participant movement remains one of shock. The adjustments do not seem to have been so radical. But this movement of consumers, far more than the admonitions of leaders and commissions, forced institutions of higher education to reexamine, clarify, and make explicit their goals as they had rarely done before.

Up until the seventies everyone seemed to believe that education was good per se and that whatever was available was good for you, whether it was what you had wanted and anticipated or not. Statistics from the Bureau of the Census in 1970 continued to document the fact that more education correlated with higher lifetime earnings (just as it still does).

A near-revolutionary idea out of the civil rights movement of the sixties had begun to cut into the accepted practice of using a degree as a requirement for a job. It was that ability to perform a job was the only fair criterion for employment; a credential such as a college degree that was closely related to a person's level of privilege in society should not be tolerated. This idea came into its own when the courts were called on to enforce equal employment opportunity for women and minority groups. Everyone began looking at what college really did to qualify one for a vocation, and as a result, the general defense of a "liberal education" as preparation for "any type of job" had to be reexamined.

Public and private colleges and universities were put under similar pressure—indirectly—by the reaction of students in proprietary schools who sometimes expected something other than what they got. Better Business Bureaus, community ombudsmen, and federal agencies responded to complaints that the instruction was not what had been promised or that jobs that were supposed to be available were not. These complaints, sometimes legitimate, encouraged students in nonprofit institutions to step forward as well.

While conferences were held on consumer rights, for some time complaints were treated by responsible college officials as nuisances created by people who really didn't understand higher education. The impact of this so-called lack of understanding on governance surfaced in one major state in 1975 when the Ohio House of Representatives sent to the Senate an appropriation act with the following statement of legislative intent:

> Among the factors which the General Assembly will use to evaluate the performance of state-assisted institutions of higher education will be the number of students served, the number of students completing an educational program for which they were enrolled, *and the placement of students in occupational positions generally related to their field of undergraduate, graduate, or professional study and training....* [italics added]

The italicized words were deleted by the Senate Finance Committee, but the cloud was clearly on the horizon. A few universities began to reeducate the persons who wrote their catalogs, and their admissions officers and counselors, to give prospective students a clear picture of what to expect. Several faculty senates protested vigorously, and everyone denounced the state coordinating board for beginning a systematic campaign to establish consumer information and protection procedures.

The basic problem was, as the Carnegie group had said, to clarify what universities and colleges really offered to the consumer. Students knew that they did not know what was behind the whole enterprise; higher education was a happy hunting ground where the free spirit—or even the cautious—might roam relatively certain that the game would be worth the chase. In this setting, the student often elevated his disappointments and irritations to the level of demands, primarily demands for right of participation. Administrators could protest that the students were transients with transient interests; faculty unions could object to third parties at the bargaining table. Everyone could agree that no students were representative of all.

Self-selection is always important, however, in the governing of any group. Some of the younger students were active, some not. For a time students in their thirties and older made themselves felt by their presence or absence; they did not sign up for unattractive packages. Then a few of them brought suit against their colleges, and a few began to join their colleagues and younger students in discussions with legislators. Before long, administrators took the initiative in devising regular ways for the disgruntled to find surcease and for the continually concerned to find a meaningful forum. The student (the consumer) became a participant in collegial governance.

In the early eighties, collegial governance was struggling with another basic issue, probably the most serious challenge in years: faculty collective bargaining. On some campuses, unionization had developed as a result of the same sort of economic issues associated with unions in manufacturing industries—compensation, working conditions, treatment of employees. On others, faculty rankled against authoritarian administrations and the failure to achieve collegial governance on academic issues. On some state university campuses faculty argued that unions would be effective in dealing with state legislatures sensitive to union membership.

Some of the goals of faculties as they unionized were achieved, but few social organizations turn out exactly as planned. Compensation issues were dealt with effectively for about five years, but union negotiators could not admit that to meet their demands the budgets for such things as libraries had to be eroded. Collegial governance was actually improved on enough campuses so that organizers could cite them as examples in their recruiting. Those who thought that generally acceptable procedures on some of the better university campuses would be improved and that union issues could be separated from more general governance were rudely awakened. As uninvolved sociologists predicted, the new organizations had lives and priorities of their own. Governing the unions presented issues beyond those of governing the academy; interunion competition encouraged leaders to move to extreme positions and made it impossible to take a broader outlook; antagonism was more functional than cooperation.

It was the faculty member who had anticipated a solution to routine problems who was most disappointed. On many campuses union negotiators began to determine the nature of the school while they were ostensibly negotiating compensation and working conditions. Faculty members found that union meetings became yet another forum demanding their attention; some woke to find that their pleasant lack of attention to detail had bound them by contract to strictures (often of their representatives' contrivance) that were more radical than those of the administration against which they had mildly protested by paying union dues.

Unions did, however, involve campuses with the legislatures. Instead of one primary voice—the president or the coordinating agency—there were now several, occasionally in harmony. In some states where formula budget allocations had been used to keep budget flexibility in the hands of the university itself, union contracts forced legislative intervention and state attention to internal allocations. This above all froze the patterns of adaptability to new challenges as far as the campus was concerned and put initiative into the hands of legislative committees.

The legislatures had opened the way for further bureaucratic participation in governance by responding to the issue that in those days was called affirmative action. Affirmative action programs, in essence, asserted the goal of equality of opportunity for each individual regardless of race, sex, national origin, or age, but defined "equality" operationally (and legally in some states) to require recruitment, placement, and promotion, so that employees (or students) would "reasonably" reflect the race and sex composition of the population. Race had been the issue that gave affirmative action its impetus in the 1960s. Before affirmative action programs were 10 years old, sexual discrimination was a matter of general concern and it gave the movement a much broader popular base.

The initial enforcement of affirmative action programs was carried out with great enthusiasm by dedicated administrators who found in the regulations weapons created by majority government to be used against the majority. University administrations bristled at first as a new-style quota system became a part of the governance structure of colleges. These quotas were not designed to limit the number of persons from special groups but to establish the minimum numbers of minorities or women.

Fortunately, a formal mechanism was eventually established to implement a program that increased opportunity for minorities and women. The agencies first moved from the impossible task of demanding that the few thousand minorities and women with professional degrees hold all the jobs in all the universities to planning and implementing faculty development programs aimed at women and minorities. This followed a recognition by universities that they had been as strong a bastion against change as any sector of society. Affirmative action administrators recognized acceptable first steps with the assurance that opportunity for women and minorities was buttressed by recruitment and support programs.

The excitement that carried the programs in their first years wore off, as it always does. It was popular to say that there was a white or male backlash against efforts by minorities and women to gain employment and equality. There was some of this, to be sure, because racial and sex discrimination were built deeply into society's attitudes and practices. But the strength of the civil rights movement generally was a sense of justice built into American mythology that could not tolerate unfair practices when they were exposed.

When the spirit of the new movement for minorities and women began to be rationalized in government agencies, some persons mistakenly thought it would lose its impact. It was not so. The idea that every opportunity was open, that any woman or any minority person could choose among infinite varieties of employment—it was this idea that fed the revolution that has given us up to 35 percent women on our faculties this year.

Another important issue for governance in the last 25 years brought everyone into the arena. Though closely related to all the other issues, it demanded a response from every party at all interested in higher education. Briefly stated it was, Who gives the stamp of approval?

For hundreds of years, it seems, college faculties had proposed what they would teach, judged the work of a student in school, and attested to his accomplishments with a degree. College trustees and administrators might privately question a faculty's judgment, but rarely did they veto a decision made through the accepted procedures. History recorded many interventions as legislators created new institutions or established required courses, as accrediting societies refused approval of new ideas, or as state agencies questioned new degree programs.

It seemed that by the 1980s the whole system was in disarray. Almost none of the traditional limitations applied to the way colleges offered their wares. Some of the problems were created by competition for students as costs rose and the traditional college-age population fell. Others were created by educational technology and by the fact that noneducators were often far more skilled in applying learning theory than college faculty.

To make the most of the available markets, colleges offered courses off their campuses almost anywhere an economically profitable group could be assembled. The apparent and real dilution of traditional quality control mechanisms attracted the concern of private accrediting agencies and pushed state agencies toward new regulatory duties. The same thing occurred as televised courses, cassettes, videotapes, and teaching machines became more popular. If they had validity in a campus learning center, they had the same validity in a student's home, but the evaluation mechanism was weaker. If a professor could prepare a program, so could a television production crew. But what "credit" would that course bring?

It is a testimony to the persistence of honor attached to a college degree that so many persons want their work similarly recognized even today. In the same years when attacks were being made on degrees as credentials, demands were made that degree credit be given for noncollegiate work. The tests now used for degrees (however a person prepares for them) were initiated then by schools and testing agencies, fought over by faculties, and hailed by journalists. But who certified the credit? From the legislators to the trustees to the faculty to the user, everyone wanted a part.

The president of a major university back in the midseventies had written of the erosion of power of his office. We have managed to restore some of the responsibilities he had in those smaller colleges with distinctive programs. We are comfortable with the new unionism; higher eduction has co-opted state coordinating boards but not the legislative committees; opportunity for all races and sexes is plentiful. But the issues of confidence and certification of quality with which that president and his successors wrestled are still with us and more persons are having their say. I wonder if it will ever change in a democratic society.

Making Prophecies
of Our Goals

Theodore M. Hesburgh

We have had only one other millennial year, 1000, in this Christian era. At that time there were dire predictions of the end of the world, wild chiliastic dreams, and all the rest. We will probably hear it again.

One would hope, however, that we have matured somewhat during the present millennium. Certainly the world is vastly different than it was in the year 1000. No one would have been discussing the future of higher education then, because we were still 200 years away from the founding of the first university in Paris. Intellectually, the ages then were dark at best, the language mainly a bastard Latin, the manuscripts few in that pre-Gutenberg age. By our standards, almost everyone, save a few clerics, was illiterate; life was culturally brutal; learning was almost nonexistent except for the preservation in monasteries of a few intellectual gems from a long-distant golden age. I speak of the Western world, the only world celebrating this particular millennium, although for our humility it should be mentioned that there were a few bright lights glowing in Asia and, strangely enough, in Mesoamerica. Despite the new and different kind of gloom that characterizes our age, and unlike those prophets of a thousand years ago crouched over flickering candles in the mountain vastness of Subiaco or Monte Cassino, I, a kind of monk like them, at least sharing their common vows of poverty, chastity, and obedience, write these lines on a yellow pad instead of parchment, with a ball-point pen instead of a quill, not in a monastery but higher than they in their mountains, traveling at 600 miles an hour in the bright, clear air.

Despite the incredible change of pace in the conditions surrounding us now as compared to then, life and learning fundamentally pose many of the same problems. They are mainly orientational problems of value, meaning, direction, attitude, ultimately salvation, now and eternally, for the many who still believe in eternity, however incoherently, no less longingly.

The year 2000, a quarter of a century away, is only one fortieth of the distance that man has come in time since the year 1000. While there will be some changes in the human condition, I would not see anything cataclysmic, barring nuclear or biological warfare. We will probably muck up the world somewhat more, but less rapidly than at present. There will be a few billion more people, but they will mostly be on the other side of the globe and in the southern hemisphere. Again, the rate of growth will have begun to level off if we have had enough sense to help them develop more humanly than at present. There will be scientific breakthroughs, though nothing as spectacular as nuclear energy, rocketry, computers, and all that they made possible in the last quarter century. Our future scientific gains will be more generally in the field of biology than in chemistry and physics, although the great gains in these latter will have facilitated the biological spectaculars yet to come. I doubt that we will have heard from other intelligent beings in the universe by the year 2000, although I have no doubt that they are there.

Against this background, it may sound banal to predict a few modest changes in the world of higher education, specifically in the United States, which happens to be the world leader in this field. First, I suspect that we will struggle to strike a better balance between equality and quality than exists at present. As a member of the Commission on Civil Rights and the Carnegie Commission on the Future of Higher Education, I pressed long and fervently for better access to higher education for those minorities so long denied equality of opportunity. While the task is still unfinished, we have succeeded beyond our initial hopes and the machinery is in place for further success. As so often happens in human affairs, the good was in some ways the enemy of the better. Equality often came at the cost of quality, funds for the latter being transferred to the former. Quality of education was also wounded in more subtle ways. Greater masses of minorities were given what often was called higher education but really was not. This is understandable, since a mere decade cannot make up for the deficiencies of centuries.

However, I would predict that wiser counsel and greater balance will prevail by the year 2000. Equality is essential to our political system and moral convictions as a nation. Yet without the highest quality of learning as a constant standard, supported concurrently and generously with equality, the higher learning will sink ever lower to the dismal level of the least common denominator. As the leader in higher education in all the world, we cannot debase its value even as we widen access to higher education. I look for a growing balance in that equation; if we do not cherish quality education and the highest standards, we will have given equal access to something not really worth having. Without high quality, education is a counterfeit and a fraud.

Secondly, I believe that higher learning will be more closely and finely focused on how to learn continually. If anything impresses one comparing the world of the last millennium to the world of the next, it is the enormous growth in what now must be learned, the explosion of knowledge, especially scientific and technological, the rate of growth with which we must cope in the learning process. I suspect the learning of the future will strike a note of intellectual curiosity, anticipation of what is yet to come, rather than simple control of present knowledge, security in the current state of the art. In the future, even starting today, students must learn to live with rapid, abrupt, and even frightening change. Learning will be correlative with life, an exciting intellectual adventure for which students will have to be explicitly prepared.

Thirdly, I voice a hope as much as a prophecy. In a world of sudden and cataclysmic change, simple sanity requires some constants. Navigation requires reasonably fixed points of reference. Without navigation, life today becomes irrational wandering, a journey with no homecoming, a voyage without a port of call, a story without meaning or ending.

Higher education in our day is weakest in this respect. Values, whether intellectual or moral, are largely characterized by their absence. Often enough, we cannot even agree on what these values should be as constants, much less how they might possibly be part of higher education. One would hope that between now and the year 2000 we might, as a means of intellectual and moral survival, begin to renew in higher education the kind of dialog that sought a higher learning in Plato's *Republic*; in Aristotle's *Ethics*; in the Old and New Testaments; in the history of saints and sinners, heroes and cowards; in the literature that so beautifully has personalized values or the lack of them in recent centuries. We should not be afraid to seek wisdom and virtue in cultures other than our own, for greatness and goodness are the same wherever they are found. They are the constants that bring quality to the whole endeavor of higher education, to the life and achievement of humankind in every age. Somehow in the welter and abruptness of change, we have lost our grip on these constants. We would all admit in the quiet of our consciences that justice is better than injustice, love better than hate, integrity better than dishonesty, compassion better than insensitivity, beauty better than ugliness, hope better than despair, faith better than infidelity, order better than chaos, peace better than war, life better than death, knowledge better than ignorance, and so on.

All these are constants that were important to the monk on the mountain and the peasant in the field in the year 1000. Whatever the enormity of our growth in knowledge and technique since then, they are still important. Without these constants, these values, we will be neither educated, nor wise, nor able to cope with change.

Lastly, I hope that higher education will challenge its students to create a rather new kind of world, characterized by quite different social, economic, and political arrangements. The emphasis will be on the interdependence rather than the independence of nation states. Students will be challenged to be world citizens as they seek solutions to problems of human rights, ecumenism, food, fuel, shelter, health care, urbanization, pollution, crime, terrorism, development, education. None of these problems has a purely national solution. They are all illustrative of the interdependence of all humankind today. No longer can geographic prejudice decree that being born in the northern hemisphere promises an infinitely more human and humane existence than being born in the southern. No longer can the affluent and powerful view the world as if everything important runs on a line between New York, London, Paris, Moscow, Peking, and Tokyo. Better than two thirds of humanity lives well south of that line and it is their earth, too. Students in the year 2000 will increasingly be made conscious of the possibility of creating a better world than the one they are inheriting, one with liberty and justice for all, not just Americans, with liberty, equality, and fraternity for all, not just Frenchmen.

Since we do not live well or even perform well in the face of abrupt discontinuities, one might hope that the value of a world view, characterized by the interdependence of all humankind, might begin to enter into the substance of higher education even now, so that the year 2000 will be a crescendo of interdependence, not a belated beginning. For the real value of looking ahead, even prophesying, is that it clarifies our present perspectives, priorities, and hopes. Before taking that step into the future, it is good to know where it will lead us so that our goal becomes our prophecy as we walk with hope and vision, even today.

VI
Epilogue

The Rest Was History

John R. Silber

From the perspective of the year 2025, it now seems obvious that 2000 was the watershed year in the history of higher education in the United States. Because it is all too easy, in the context of higher education's current prestige and affluence, to forget the travails that led up to the second millennium, I propose briefly to summarize the history of what was called postsecondary education during the last quarter of the twentieth century.

The educators of 1976 peered into the future through an opening flanked by two immense figures. Standing like the pillars of Hercules, Herman Kahn and Colonel Blimp symbolized the duality inherent in planning—pretension and error. (Colonel Blimp's bumbling made him the most popular futurist, preferred not merely for a confessed incompetence that had become especially appealing in a completely egalitarian society but also for his principled avoidance of linear extrapolations.)

Although many observers in 1976 believed that faculty unionization was the wave of the future, no one foresaw the titanic struggle for the allegiance of academics that erupted following the demise of the AAUP and the NEA between the Teamsters and the revived Industrial Workers of the World; nor that its outcome would be the supplanting of "Gaudeamus Igitur" by "Joe Hill" as the unofficial alma mater and drinking song of all universities.

Once university administrators learned that General Motors shared little if any administrative authority with the United Auto Workers, and that the industrial model allowed such fiscal conveniences as the laying off of temporarily redundant faculty, there were few professors who did not look back with nostalgia to those bad old days of collegiality. The profound and inbred conservatism of most academics kept them from admitting this; indeed, the less happy they became with their hard-won, blue-collar status, the more likely they were to wear hard hats and blue collars and to carry lunch pails as they entered their academic factories.

The new egalitarianism, which taught that there must be not only equality of access to higher education but also equality of result, developed rapidly after 1976. Behavioral objectives and competence-based programs were instrumental in this development: Once it was decided that the time it took to learn something was irrelevant to learning, it was possible for medical students who took five years to master organic chemistry not only to practice alongside their fleeter colleagues, but also to buy the same no-fault malpractice insurance. By century's end, a movement arose to rid higher education of its speciesism—its exclusive preoccupation with the education of human beings. The Department of General Welfare ruled that the fact that a dog took 10 weeks to learn to shake hands (one of the basic requirements for a doctorate under reforms introduced in 1984) must not be held against it. The important thing, GW argued, was the dog's eventual competence.

From this development it was a short step to the generalized doctrine that any educational program made available to one species must be made available to all. Having ruled that performance is all, GW began to withhold federal funds from any program in marine biology that did not provide for the education as well as the study of dolphins.

Although the conversion of equal opportunity into equal credentialing increased the admissions pool slightly, it could not fully counteract the enrollment decline that resulted inevitably from the sharply decreased freshman classes that began arriving after 1978. Politicians in general persisted in believing the superstition that independent colleges and universities were private, and they allocated comparatively little aid to the independent sector. By the end of the century the independent sector consisted of about 30 heavily endowed institutions and a handful of religious foundations. The state sector was not immune to the effects of declining enrollment, but most of its institutions—the largest ones—survived. (The average institution of higher learning in 1990 enrolled 17,500 students while the largest single campus enrolled 100,000. Only three campuses remained in the United States with student bodies under 1,500.)

The status of postsecondary education at the turn of the century was extraordinarily low. Bills had been introduced in many states to confer the bachelor's degree as an incident of passing the driver's license examination, and several universities were planning to make the professoriat hereditary. (In order to avoid constitutional obstacles, the doctrine of primogeniture was assiduously avoided in the development of hereditary entitlements.) The outlook was grim, but help was on the way.

On July 4, 1976 (unknown to anyone else at the time), researchers funded by the Center for the Study of Democratic Institutions, working in a laboratory in the subbasement of the University of Chicago library (on the site of its abandoned football stadium), had successfully cloned Robert Maynard Hutchins. RMH-2, as he was known, was carefully raised in a modified Skinner box at the Center. At the age of 24, RMH-2 was deemed ready to leave the box and undertake a university presidency. That he should have been comparatively more precocious than his celebrated clonemate (who was 29 when he assumed the law deanship at Yale and 30 when he became president of the University of Chicago) was attributed to the fact that the younger generation is always better than its predecessor. The same argument was advanced to explain his additional three inches in height.

In the fall term of 2000-2001, RMH-2 was set down with 20,000 students in the formerly small village of New Bologna, Wisconsin, and told to operate the most exotic and innovative university that he could imagine. His first act was to discover that about half of his prospective students had neither interest in, nor capacity for, further education. Rejoicing, he sent them home, rejoicing. He next restored the archaic term "higher education," realizing that the term "postsecondary education" had been devised by those who had no answer to the question, "Higher than what?" He then issued, under his own name, RMH-2, a new printing of RMH-1's *The Higher Learning in America*. (It had been established in 1986 that clonemates have community property rights, and in any event, the Supreme Court, in the Xerox case of 1982, had ruled that all copyright law, being in fundamental violation of the First Amendment, was null and void.) Writing in the *New York Times*, Benjamin DeMott hailed RMH-2's new book as "the freshest and most profoundly innovative look at higher education in many years."

The rest is history.